renovating the mind

renovating the mind

experiencing God's truth
through mental renewal

abdullah birdsong

ROYAL HOUSE PRESS
An Imprint of Rhema Release Media, LLC
7504 East Independence Blvd, Suite 112
Charlotte, NC 28227

www.royalhouse.co

ISBN-10   0979446627
ISBN-13   978-0979446627

acknowledgements

First and foremost, thank you to my Heavenly Father for making this offering to the Body of Christ possible. It is by His grace that I am able to articulate His desires through written word.

I thank God for my awesome family who provided unwavering support and encouragement throughout this process. Even in seasons of loss, I was actually gaining. For their love and care, I am eternally grateful.

To the best church family in the world-Dunamis Church. Thank you for being open to the Word of God and its power to change your lives. You are a beautiful reflection and expression of God's love in the earth. It is a joy to serve as your leader.

To my God-given, anointed, and appointed wife, Marcia. Your prayers and support have been a constant source of strength to me. We have laughed and cried together many times during the creation of this work. You are a woman who fears God and I am the better for it. Thank you for loving me into my purpose and praying me into my destiny. You are an incredible mother to our son, Samuel. This book is dedicated to you.

in memoriam

Jennifer Pharris Pritchett

Charlie Mae Pharris

I heard a voice out of Heaven, "Write this: Blessed are those who die in the Master from now on; how blessed to die that way!"

"Yes," says the Spirit, "and blessed rest from their hard, hard work. None of what they've done is wasted; God blesses them for it all in the end."

Revelation 14: 13
The Message

contents

introduction

Don't copy the behavior and customs of this world, but let God transform you into a new person by changing the way you think. Then you will learn to know God's will for you, which good and pleasing and perfect (Romans 12: 2 NLT).

Reading this book marks the beginning of a wonderful journey toward freedom in God. You have been fearfully and wonderfully made-designed by the Master to live in joy, peace, and righteousness.

I believe that to experience true freedom, a person must be willing to change they way they think and perceive their surroundings. Changing the way we think inherently changes the thoughts that influence what we say and how we act.

Even if the lenses we view life through are influenced by situations we've experienced, we still have a responsibility to make sure those are the lenses God desires us to see through. To accurately correct vision problems an optometrist must diagnose the problem to offer a viable solution.

This book serves as a means for you to diagnose if your thought-life is the one God desires. If it isn't, don't despair. The Holy Spirit is available to lead, guide, instruct, and encourage you during the journey. God has promised to never leave you. You have an all-powerful partner whose expertise is showing unconditional love. When we are weak He is strong. I guarantee that as you draw closer to Him, He will draw closer to you. God's desire is that you grow exponentially in Christ during the process of mental renovation. No matter where you are in life, no matter the status you've achieved, you are still a prime candidate for the blessing God has when the renovation is completed.

It is my prayer that you will think, see, feel, realize, conceptualize, visualize, prioritize, and operate on a higher-level as a result of experiencing this book.

I encourage you to read through this book with a Bible close by and a pen or highlighter handy. As you turn the pages God, by His Spirit will nudge and nourish your mind with knowledge, wisdom, and insight. He will speak. Be ready to listen.

The mental renovation process can be summed up as a series of positive changes to the way you think. These changes, undertaken in partnership with the Holy Spirit, yield a transformation that unleashes God's revelation of truth. This revelation serves as the basis for learning and operating in His will and as assurance that everything that God does in you is good, pleasing, and perfect.

Abdullah Birdsong

chapter one
the ultimate upgrade

The widely quoted adage of the United Negro College Fund reminds us that, "a mind is a terrible thing to waste." This statement is also applicable to the thought life of a follower of Jesus Christ. As believers, we exist in a temporal world. All that surrounds us has a beginning and ending point. Time waits for no one. The world's first dominion-oriented creature, Adam, created by God, exhibited an eternalness that was eventually destroyed by sin. Because satan persuaded Eve to disobey God's command, their descendants (mankind) were made captive to a sinful nature. Consequently, we are temporal. Over time, our bodies eventually slow down and our getting older is a gradual movement toward the end of our earthly existence. At some point time on earth will end and believers will join God in heaven—the unrepentant will spend eternity in hell. Our less-than-perfect existence dictates that we all will, at one time or another, have need of renewal or renovation.

Anything in constant use eventually shows signs of wear and tear. Some instances dictate that vital components may need to be replaced while others need only to be refurbished or renovated. Your mind is one of the components of who you are that must consistently be refreshed and rejuvenated.

Our minds constantly process the world around us. Opportunities abound to ponder and process worldly distractions rather thanspiritual things. Actually, we have more time to mediate on spiritual things, if we so choose. Joshua 1:8 says,

> Study this Book of the Law continually. Meditate on it day and night so you may be sure to obey all that is written in it. Only then will you succeed.

So, if you study, mediate, and obey His Word then you will have no choice but to succeed.

Consider our society and the Church. It often seems as if the Body of Christ is light years behind today's culture. Perhaps this is because we haven't given serious enough thought to the things of God. It is possible to honor ritualistic procedures over the presence and power of God. To reclaim it's rightful authority, the Church must position itself to give due attention to the desires of God's heart, not man-made desires and fantasies.

You might ask, "Why another book on the mind?" True, there are numerous treatises for the hungry reader to choose from. The answer is simple. Your mind has much to do with how and what you think. Your thinking has much to do with making decisions. Your decisions have much to do with how you act and respond. Your mind is the hub of all your actions. Your actions have much to do with your life. And finally, your life has much to do with your destiny. Consequently, it is in the mind that we fight our most violent battles with the forces of evil. So, renovating your mind is serious business. Anyone can benefit from a God-ordained change in the way they think.

Since God has great things for you to accomplish, your mind must be renovated. Your mental upgrade must occur, and quickly, so you can sustain a life that gives God glory and serves to benefit the causes of Christ. You qualify for this ultimate upgrade because of God's sacrificial act. Jesus Christ endured unbelievable amounts of ridicule and the suffering of the cross so that we can live in freedom and victory. This victory in Jesus is not a far-fetched notion. It is a very present, now-time reality. The victorious life is possible and sustainable with a mind free from the influence and torment of satan.

The Upgrade

Let's say you purchased new software for your computer and were very excited the first few days you explored its capabilities. The software was a hefty, but worthwhile, investment so you continued to use it faithfully. You made the purchase because you believed it would make your life easier. As expected, it increased your efficiency and productivity. Behind the scenes, there are people who work for the software company, spending late hours endeavoring to improve the software you purchased. A few months pass and you learn that the software has an available upgrade. The manufacturer suggests that all users take advantage of the upgrade to experience additional functionality. The software even reminds you when an upgrade is available because you took the time to register your purchase. Being "registered" with God allows the Holy Spirit to remind you of your need of an upgrade from Him.

You momentarily halt work and download the upgrade. Typically, the speed of your Internet connection determines whether the process will take minutes or hours. You receive the upgrade and then use the software with its new features and added security. Life is great, or at least less stressful, because you took the time to download the enhancement.

In essence, that is what renovating your mind is all about—taking time out of your busy schedule to receive a download from God to prepare you to be more effective in His purpose for your life. Receiving a download from God equips and empowers you to put down your load-those things, people, and situations that plague your life and attempt to rob you of the significance you were created to operate with. That's why having a good connection, a two-way means of communication, with God is vitally important. How quickly your mental renovation is accomplished is largely dependent on your type of connection.

The Need For Speed

In large, our culture offers high-speed connectivity to many things. Fast food, fast worship, fast paced life. Contemporary culture also, whether intentionally or not, simultaneously promotes a low-tech, dial-up connection to God. God has many things He desires to get to us fast, but often our connection speed slows the process. When operating with a slow connection to God, we tend to concentrate more on the lure of physical and emotional comfort than on Godly principles for abundant living.

By and large mainstream culture does not operate according to God's principles. Many people profess to be Christians, but on their own terms. Typically, people don't submit themselves to a mindset that suggests or even promotes God-ordained mental renovation. We are too busy and if given a choice we would probably stay too busy. The majority of American Christians believe that a weekly trip to church equates to a sure entrance into Heaven. If a person goes to church regularly and tries to do the right thing most of the time they are a shoe-in for Heaven, right? In reality, attendance at weekly worship experiences are but a small portion of what God requires from us. Genesis 1:26 says:

> And God said, "Let us make man in our own image, in our likeness, and let them rule over the fish of the sea and the birds of the air, over the livestock, over all the earth, and over all the creatures that move along the ground." (NIV)

4

Essentially, God created you to communicate with Him so you could represent Him to the world. God, the Trinity, didn't say, "let us maybe make man in our image." No, He was so serious about making reflections of Himself, He made sure that He was in agreement with Himself! The beginning of the God's quote says, "let us." That means God, in consultation with His other two personifications, the Son and Holy Spirit, was in agreement about mankind. Jesus Christ and the Holy Spirit, are both with God from before the beginning began and were totally invested in what God spoke into existence.

Excuses, Excuses, Excuses

So, why don't more people subscribe and submit to God's process of mental renovation? Here are some reasons or assertions I commonly hear:

- "I don't know what to expect."
- "I'm not very religious."
- "People won't understand me anymore."
- "Maybe later. Right now I'm enjoying life too much."
- "I'm not into all that suffering with Christ stuff."
- "My relationship with God is my personal business."

There are four reasons why many people don't take the chance to change for the better.

- They fear living a life without purpose.
- They fear being alone.
- They fear being lost and dealing with the unknown.
- They fear that they would die in the process.

In my ministry experiences I have heard all of the above. Perhaps the two most significant fears people possess concerning renovating their mind are of being alone and being lost. However, there is an awesome newness on the other side of the process. In reality, not many things in life are easy. There's no such thing as a free lunch. Whether you desire to loose weight or skydive, the process has its associated risks and costs. Dieting, discipline, or training for that new career all have a price. At the outset the process might seem overwhelming. Maybe you have never allowed God to perform this higher degree of His work in you before now. You must overcome all fear and grow in God's grace. Trust God to work His plan for your life. Jazz trumpeter W.C. Handy once said, "Life is something like a trumpet. If you don't put anything in, you won't get anything out."

Worth the Risk

A worthwhile renovation is not an easy undertaking. The homeowner who undertakes an expansive renovation will most likely experience periods of discomfort or inconvenience because normal home-based activities must be altered to allow the process to be completed. Likewise, life must also adjust to accommodate the process of change. If it means using a secondary bathroom while the one in the master suite is being overhauled-then so be it.

Unlike the efforts of "weekend warriors," the task of renovating the mind is not to be undertaken alone, and can't be completed in a couple of days. What makes a well-done renovation worth the while is it's potential for adding value and making a new level of living possible.

Partners In Progress

The process of renovating the mind must be a partnership between you and God. Yes, God could do it all by Himself, but, you'll appreciate the experience more if you have a vested interest. Your sweat equity is necessary since "faith without works is dead." (James 2:26) You can't go about business as usual and expect a spiritual breakthrough. It is foolish to think you can consistently do the same thing and get different results.

The renovation commences only after a conscious decision is made to better yourself. Renovating your mind requires discipline and patience. The rewards are far more awesome than you could ever imagine. There's comfort in knowing that all things work out for those who love God and work according to His purpose.

A Faith-Based Initiative

Renovating the mind is a faith-based initiative. The term *faith* has simply this meaning: to believe and rely upon. There probably will be times when it seems as nothing adds up. In those times defer to God. To *defer* means to yield in judgment and opinion. God has all the answers. In fact, He knew all your questions and their answers before you were formed in your mother's womb (Jeremiah 1:5). He knew exactly what difficulties you would experience. Life will not give you what you desire or even deserve. Life will give you what you settle for. Therefore, it is extremely important that Proverbs 3:5 be applied to life's tough situations. Trust in God with all your heart and lean not unto your own understanding. When situations don't make sense, don't panic. God makes perfect sense of everything and arranges all things to the benefit of those who love Him.

Don't attempt to renovate your mind with a preplanned agenda. In Proverbs 3:7 we are instructed to, "be not wise in our own eyes." Allow the Holy Spirit to lead and guide every step along this journey. This renovation experience requires dedicated willingness to set aside your will and allow God, via His Spirit, to begin and sustain this powerful work in your life. God will take the lead, if you allow.

How does this partnership with God work? First, remember that God is three in one: Father, Son, and Holy Spirit. God is one with three personifications or personalities. Each aspect of God has a role to play in your renovation.

Think of God the Father as the Chief Architect and General Contractor. Jesus Christ, God the Son, is the material from which any structure should be erected. Lastly, you and the Holy Spirit are co-subcontractors. Once you submit to God's call for the renovation of your mind, He gets to work on His master drawings. God the Father then works to rearrange, broaden, enhance, and update your thought life. After revealing the blueprints, He enacts His vision by giving general oversight to the entire process.

It's Demolition Time

A renovation project normally begins with the removal of old material and debris. Homeowners, and their contractors, typically elect to rent a large receptacle to ensure that the disposal of debris is handled according to local law. I have witnessed renovations where the contractor carelessly discarded debris around the worksite. The mess became an occupational hazard, eyesore, as well as a sign of a lack of professionalism.

Conversely, God does all things well and with a spirit of excellence. You don't have to worry about God leaving a mess. Even as mental renovation is occurring He desires that you prosper and be in good health. This prosperity is not the result of anything you bring to the table. The process is bankrolled by God's grace and mercy. Even though it looks and feels like you are stripped bare, God makes sure that every onlooker knows that the renovation is in great hands. After all, the site of the work, which represents you, is being handled with utmost care and excellence. He makes sure to place a beautiful sign on site, like any excellent contractor should, that gives people something to look forward to when the work is done.

If you haven't asked God to demolish the old un-renovated you, now is a good time. A major reason a structure is deemed condemned is because of the foundation. If the foundation is not laid properly the entire structure will eventually become unstable. Buildings that remain unstable for extended periods of time are eventually abandoned and condemned. They are condemned to protect those in the vicinity. The lack of adequate care and maintenance causes structures to fall into disrepair. They soon become infested with all sorts of undesirable inhabitants.

Unlike the structure I just mentioned, if Christ is truly your Lord and Savior then you cannot be condemned for any reason. God is always willing and ready to fix you up. Romans 8:1-2 says,

> So now there is no condemnation for those who belong to Christ Jesus. And because you belong to him, the power of the life-giving Spirit has freed you from the power of sin that leads to death.

The purpose of mental demolition is to draw you into God's revelation of who He is. God does His best work when we are broken and in need of repair. It's okay to be broken when you know God's going to be repairing you.

"Who Do You Say That I Am?"

In Matthew 16:13-20 we find Jesus initiating conversation with His disciples by asking a question:

When Jesus came into the coasts of Caesarea Philippi, he asked his disciples, saying, Whom do men say that I the Son of man am? And they said, Some *say that thou art* John the Baptist: some, Elias; and others, Jeremias, or one of the prophets. He saith unto them, But whom say ye that I am? And Simon Peter answered and said, Thou art the Christ, the Son of the living God. And Jesus answered and said unto him, Blessed art thou, Simon Barjona: for flesh and blood hath not revealed *it* unto thee, but my Father which is in heaven. And I say also unto thee, That thou art Peter, and upon this rock I will build my church; and the gates of hell shall not prevail against it. And I will give unto thee the keys of the kingdom of heaven: and whatsoever thou shalt bind on earth shall be bound in heaven: and whatsoever thou shalt loose on earth shall be loosed in heaven. Then charged he his disciples that they should tell no man that he was Jesus the Christ. (KJV)

Jesus already knew who they were. However, He was interested to find out if they knew Him. Notice immediately that the disciples began reporting what others assumed about Jesus. The un-renovated mind attempts to play tricks on us because it's filled with what others have said about who Jesus is. The disciples were no longer spring chickens. They had been with Jesus for a while. They should have known who He was.

Jesus was approaching his crucifixion and desired to clarify two major issues with those who followed him. First was the issue of who He was. Second, and most importantly, what He was about to do. When we embrace the truths about Jesus and His sacrificial act we embark on an experience of purposeful growth in our thinking and perception of our surroundings. Indeed, the disciples were human. Their minds were filled with a mixture of Christ's agenda and their personal struggles. When confronted with the all-important question of Jesus' identity, the disciples exhibited various viewpoints. None except Simon Peter's was accurate.

Our thought processes weigh heavily upon our viewpoint or stance on an issue. If you constantly have negative thoughts, that's the lens you tend to view the world through. Constantly negative people tend to harbor dark thoughts. On the other hand, Jesus is the light of the world, our hope eternal. Many miss out on what God has for them because of misguided perceptions and viewpoints. The corresponding attitudes and dispositions produced by negative thinking exclude them from experiencing the fullness of God. Romans 8:5-8 says,

> Those who are dominated by the sinful nature think about sinful things, but those who are controlled by the Holy Spirit think about things that please the Spirit. So letting your sinful nature control your mind leads to death. But letting the Spirit control your mind leads to life and peace. For the sinful nature is always hostile to God. It never did obey God's laws, and it never will. That's why those who are still under the control of their sinful nature can never please God.

An Ex-Negative

I confess, I am an ex-negative person. God has opened my eyes to how warped, misguided viewpoints caused many unnecessary problems for me and those I loved. After realizing the awful atmosphere I had created, I vowed to never be bound to accepting the worst-case scenario of any situation again.

Allow me to give you an example of how detrimental my thinking used to be. While driving in inclement weather I would allow myself to be plagued by thoughts of having a terrible accident. According to my un-renovated way of thinking, the idea of dying "accidentally" seemed like a constantly viable option. I was inviting tragedy into my life because of bad thinking. I tended to make simple mistakes when stressed. Any mistake in those conditions could have been detrimental. If my mind had been consumed with the things of God, I would have no time to consider such nonsense. Fortunately, God's grace was working in my life because I never had the accident I dreaded.

Likewise the disciples of Jesus, in their humanity, fell prey to the same warped thinking we experience today. At the Last Supper, instead of internalizing the words of the Master, they quarreled about who was the greatest disciple. They were too concerned about what others were saying. The disciples had become people pleasers instead of God-pleasers. Their thoughts were not His thoughts therefore their ways were far from His ways. Peter, James, John and the rest were there to learn from Jesus, not to vie against each other for position in the Kingdom. It pays immeasurable dividends to learn from the Master. If they truly understood the promise of God manifested through Jesus Christ, they would have been more prepared for what lied ahead. Jesus was demonstrating a Kingdom principle that whoever is enthused about serving others would be greatly rewarded by the His Father.

Learn From the Best

Learning is an essential part of any maturation process. During the course of our life on earth we are exposed to both good and bad instruction. Keep in mind that God desires for you to dwell richly in all knowledge. A wise man will increase his understanding by hearing (Proverbs 1:5). The Bible speaks profoundly of God's desire for us to be well educated. Typically, learning can be divided into two broad categories: experiential and academic.

Learning From Experience

Experiential learning is circumstantial and societal in

nature. We learn by living in and interacting with the world around us. It is possible to gain a great deal of practical knowledge without formal education. Some would call that "street sense." Many of our ancestors didn't have the privilege of attending prestigious epicenters of learning like Oxford University, Harvard, or Morehouse College. They learned about God and His love for them by faith. They lived out their salvation day by day while dealing with the good, bad, and the ugly. I surmise that a wealth of wisdom lies in our "griots"-those with a historical story to tell. Noted educator Vivian Gadsden shares a powerful story about learning:

> My father completed only about four years of formal schooling. His school was a one-room classroom that he, his four brothers, and his two sisters attended. By the time my father was in what was considered to be fourth grade, he had learned as much as his older siblings who had stopped attending school to help with farming chores at home. In an attempt to escape the harsh discipline of his stepmother when he was about 12 years old, he and an older brother ran away from home to live with an adult sister in Philadelphia. By the time he arrived, school was but a distant memory. He kept up his reading with the newspaper every day and the Bible every night.

In biblical times parents were directly responsible for their child's education. A father was to be especially influential in the child's physical, emotional, and spiritual development. Additionally, the teacher or Rabbi, was responsible for the spiritual impartation of truth. This truth shaped the student's thinking and gradually developed a sense of morality. A return to this system of learning would be beneficial to our culture today. I disagree with the idiom that it takes a village to raise a child. Instead, I suggest that it takes a prepared, fully-invested, sacrificial, God-led village to raise a child. In our "every man for himself" culture a return to this system of community learning, where educators, parents, and the religious community collaborate, would be beneficial.

Learning From The Books

The second type of learning requires a more systematic approach. In 2 Kings 2: 3-7, Elijah is embarking on his farewell journey. He is at the end of his life and assignment for God. Elijah's prized student and constant companion Elisha is about to receive a "double portion" of the anointing God had placed on him. Before any of the aforementioned occurs, Elijah travels through Bethel, Gilgal, and Jericho. Each of the three cities included a school for the training of prophets. In these schools, a great of learning took place between mentor and student. The mentor was expected to pour out, or literally empty himself, into the life of the student. This exchange resulted in the student eventually eclipsing the mentor's impact and effectiveness. Every subsequent generation was expected to be and do more. Every student was required to be well versed in scripture and the traditions of the Old Testament prophets of times past.

No matter your experience with the process of learning, the enemy seeks to pervert it and use it for his benefit and your detriment. There are a number of well-educated people who have fallen by the wayside because their educated, academic minds were swayed from God's truth. Mental breakdowns are becoming more frequent among America's brightest and most innovative thinkers. Why is this so? Satan is an expert manipulator and distorter. Everything that looks good, feels good, tastes good, and smells good is not necessarily good. Also, it is interesting to note that satan has no creative power. His authority is limited only to the manipulation of what God has already created.

Permission To Challenge

Job was an upright and educated man who fell on hard times because God allowed him to be tested. Imagine being at the top of your game and suddenly loosing everything. Satan could do anything he wanted to Job except tamper with his soul. As the story goes, Job looses everything, but refuses to curse God. People have cursed God and lost their minds for much less than Job encountered. Job probably didn't fully understand his season of demolition. It's hard to fathom that Job lost what he did with great joy. Job was crushed. He felt forsaken. He questioned God. Nevertheless, he recognized that, in the ultimate scheme of things, God was in total control. Job's God-ordained season of reconstruction led to his supernatural restoration-double of that which he had before. I would imagine that, after being restored, Job received twice as much joy and peace also. Sometimes God subtracts so He can add.

When Things Don't Make Sense

One of satan's most profound traps is his suggestion that we must understand everything about God. Sadly, people loose their minds and relationships with God as they attempt to rationalize His every move. They end up questioning God over and over in an effort to discover answers.

The truth is that God won't totally reveal himself to us because in our imperfect human state of being we can't handle the full revelation. Instead, as believers we have the opportunity to gain adequate understanding of God by opening our eyes and hearts to His Word. In this fact, we are not alone. Many during the time of Jesus, as we do today, had difficulty seeing clearly.

> But though he had done so many miracles before them, yet they believed not on him: That the saying of Esaias the prophet might be fulfilled, which he spake, Lord, who hath

believed our report? and to whom hath the arm of the Lord been revealed? Therefore they could not believe, because that Esaias said again, He hath blinded their eyes, and hardened their heart; that they should not see with *their* eyes, nor understand with *their* heart, and be converted, and I should heal them. These things said Esaias, when he saw his glory, and spake of him (John 12: 37-41, KJV).

To our detriment, we often allow circumstances to blind us. I have issues, you have issues, we all have issues. It's these issues and our approach to them that determines our aptitude to hear and experience God. We have all failed at something, but we are not failures. How you respond to failure determines how successful you will become afterward. If you develop and retain a defeatist attitude you will continually and perpetually be defeated. On the other hand, if you treat failure as a learning experience, the rebound back into positive productivity happens naturally.

When things don't make sense the best mental position to be found in is an attitude and aptitude for listening. Be preoccupied, not with performing your normal routine, but with being still and listening. "Well, since God is not saying much, I'll just go ahead with what I've been doing." Is what you've *been* doing killing you? Is it creating distance between you and God's purpose for your life?

Many things God says or does won't make sense until we learn to walk by faith. God wants to see if we will step out on nothing and believe something is there. What is faith? I believe the hallmark definition is found in Hebrew 11:1:

Now faith is the substance of things hoped for, the evidence of things not seen. (KJV)

If you have to see it to believe it that's not faith. Faith is not concerned with believing in the impossible, it's occupied

16

with relying on the provision of Him who can do the impossible easily.

When things don't add up, don't allow satan to coax you into trying rationalize the why, when, where, how, and who. Keep in mind that satan wants to wear you down mentally. He's counting on you being no good for Kingdom work. Learn to view tough times as training for the next level instead of punishment from God. The reason you're where you are right now is because God wants you there.

From time to time God calls "time out," reducing us to our least common denominator by factoring out the ugly in our lives. The best candidates for a mental renovation are those who realize they are broken and need fixing up

The Best Material

Because God loves us, He has reserved the choicest material for our mental renovation. Jesus, the Chief Cornerstone, who was severely rejected by un-renovated minds, is incorporated into the process, and visible change commences. "But the Word is very near you, in your mouth and in your mind *and* in your heart, so that you can do it" (Deuteronomy 30:14).

It is important to keep the Word of God in your mouth, mind, and heart so that you can accomplish what He has for you to do. In Deuteronomy 30:14 the word order is intriguing. The first place God's Word should reside is the mouth. The mouth is a powerful instrument that either builds up or tears down. Also, the mouth can't build and destroy at the same time. In Job 22:28 we discover that, as believers, we can "decree a thing" and it shall be set up in our lives. The King James Version of the Bible uses the word, *established*. In Job 22:28 it is used as a verb of action. Some synonyms for *established* in this context are: to institute, start, create, begin, and launch. In essence, there are wonderful new beginnings for anyone who decrees God's will for their life. Positive declaration is one of the most powerful weapons we have at our disposal.

The second area the Word must be kept is the mind. After you have spoken the Word to yourself and others repeatedly it becomes engrained in your thinking. The mind feeds the mouth. There is no such thing as not thinking before speaking. Every word that proceeds from the mouth is first a thought.

The 2:1 Principle

Making great strides in the Kingdom is possible if we think twice before speaking once. If we took the time to seriously consider the consequences of what we say, there would be a lot less hurt and pain in the world. Just as a competent contractor measures twice then cuts once, so should we as people assigned by God to build His Kingdom. In essence, allow others to experience Jesus through what you are. Speak positive life-giving words, experience the love and mercy of God, become a recipient of the favor of God.

Some time ago I counseled a young woman. I sensed that she wanted to be free from the mindset that had maintained her bondage. She explained that she had been through "hell" several times and was ready to change. The woman had lost both parents tragically and had become the sole provider for her family. This huge responsibility had drained her mentally, physically, and emotionally.

Soon after our sessions began she shared with me her addiction to marijuana. When I asked her reason for smoking she responded that it calmed her and allowed for reflection. After listening to her, the Holy Spirit led me to ask her a series of questions. After even more conversation, I discovered what the root of the issue was. Satan had taken her mind captive and convinced her that smoking dope was perfectly okay! The devil, a specialist in issuing pain and suffering, had convinced the woman that numbing all pain was absolutely necessary. In reality, although while "high" she didn't feel physical pain, her mental pain was ever deepening because of her dependence on drugs.

Never think the enemy is after just you. He wants your heritage and your future. Because smoking dope was comfortable to the woman, her entire household began smoking and formed habits of dependency. In other words, others were assimilated into a habit because of her example.

That young woman came to the realization that more prayer and counseling was needed. Admitting that she had a problem made her a prime candidate for deliverance. In order for deliverance to occur a change of perspective was required. She had to develop a serious attitude regarding the pursuit of God's promises for her; which she eventually did.

In the New Testament the Apostle John writes to Gaius whom he sincerely loves. John blesses Gaius by desiring that he would prosper and be in good health, even as his soul prospers (3 John 2). Our Heavenly Father desires none but the same for us. That's the essence of renovating the mind. With God's help you can change your mind and condition it to focus on things that please God. Don't be intimidated by the process. God has everything under control.

The third area the Word should be kept is the heart. A man's heart is where his priorities, or treasures, reside (Matt. 6:21). It is a conflict of interest to have a dirty, broken down mind and clean heart. A clean heart is a direct product of a clear and God-ward mind. Genesis 6:5-6 proclaims:

> And God saw that the wickedness of man *was* great in the earth, and that every imagination of the thoughts of his heart *was* only evil continually. And it repented the Lord that he had made man on the earth, and it grieved him at his heart. (KJV)

Why would the thoughts of a man's heart be important to God? Look closely at what wicked ways of men caused God to do. He repented. In this context the word *thoughts* translates as mental conception, fantasy, image, or mental picture. Do you spend more time fantasizing about ungodly things than dreaming about your own God-given destiny?

Our mental conceptions must always line up with the will of God. It's easy for a flesh-driven, individual to fathom things contrary to God. However, you are a spirit that has a soul that lives in a body. Every aspect of who you are must be called into subjection to Jesus Christ so God can perform His work in you.

Tearing Down Even More

Any substantial renovation involves the tearing down or stripping away of old material to allow for the installation of new, more efficient spaces. For example, when remodeling a kitchen, a good designer studies the floor plan to determine the best use of space. He then passes that information on to the contractor. All involved parties understand that some changes will be minor while others will require extensive revamping or additional construction.

It is not wise to haphazardly begin a mental renovation. Any work of this scale and magnitude benefits from careful consideration. There is a definite thought process involved. The preliminary work of mental renovation should include prayer and praise. Only after this pre-work has been completed can the renovation commence.

We must always approach God in prayer. Prayer gets His attention because He loves to communicate with us. Keep in mind that after the product, your renovated mind, has been revealed, then freedom and promotion will be manifested!

Satan has been enjoying his attempts to ruin your life. He

desires to pervert your thought process because it is with the mind that we interpret, dream, learn, and decide. In the next chapter let's examine each of these aspects of mental function and how satan attempts to steer us away from God's desires and purpose for our lives.

A Blessed Assurance

There is absolutely no man, woman, event, circumstance, nor spirit that can single-handedly cause you to fall from God's grace. We make the decisions that shape our relationship with God. The sum of our decisions defines our lifestyle and spiritual maturity. I.V. Hilliard suggests that the development of mental toughness causes us to make purposefully accurate decisions on a consistent basis, which in turn produce success in life. God never forces us to choose good over evil. He doesn't override our will.

It is my assignment from God to, through this book, deposit in you knowledge and wisdom for your information and practical application. Make the most of these moments. Investing yourself into this process of mental renovation will reap big time dividends.

chapter two
don't lie to yourself

Keep me from lying to myself; give me the privilege of knowing your instructions - Psalm 119:29

Lying is sin and satan is the father of lies. In the Bible those who willfully deceive others are called his children. Maybe you have heard sermons about the toll lying, cheating, and deception takes on a person spiritually and physically. Despite exposure to what God says about lying, people make excuses like, "I just told a little one," or the proverbial "I was just trying to help." Lies never help, they harm. In fact lying does more harm to the liar than those he or she deceives with the lie.

The world around us has made being untruthful profitable and popular. Some find it rather comfortable to lie about everything from their age to their relationships with others. Some even deceive others about their relationship with God. They masquerade around like nothing is wrong. Like life is easy and they are immune to struggle and strain. You might know a few people like this. They are experts on everyone else's problems. But deep down inside their soul is being ravaged by unresolved inner turmoil. They become experts at hiding their hurts from others. However, the biggest liars don't lie to others as much as they lie to themselves. Answer the following questions:

- Do you give inaccurate information about any aspect of your life?

- Do you make excuses for unrighteousness in yourself or others?

- Do you do or buy things out of pure desire without seeking direction from God?

- Do you think that living in holiness before God is too difficult?

I was a liar. Years ago, I created an aura about myself that was rooted in what I wanted others to see. I was spreading untruths and living untruthfully with myself. My masterful ability to lie to others began only after a pattern of deception had taken root inside me. In other words, those who mislead others most likely have already misled themselves.

Consider an unmarried couple that decides to move in with each other. When asked why the decision was made to cohabitate they respond, "we moved in together to save money." In fact, money was not sole reason for the decision. Often people are too ashamed to disclose the real reason behind their decision. Could their agreement have one of physical or sexual convenience?

What about the gentleman who, even though it's beyond his financial means, purchases an expensive sports car? He reasons that it's a good purchase because of the plethora of safety features and outstanding warranty. There's even the Bluetooth wireless connection to help prevent mishaps while talking on the cell phone. He feels a like a responsible citizen because he is contributing to a decrease in DWT (Driving While Talking) accidents. Then there is the laser-guided cruise control to help him maintain a safe speed. There are even those trusty Xenon headlights that light up the night a quarter of a mile ahead, protecting him from any potential road hazards.

From the onset he probably won't tell you that his purchase was an ill-fated attempt to look and feel better. Maybe he just wants to feel more significant and important. Because the purchase was not made in God's perfect timing, he will probably experience financial hardship within a few months. God's blessings, given in God's timing, have staying power. You'll never have to give up what God gives.

The Benefit of Truth

These two scenarios above are not hypothetical. They are real. You probably know someone who could benefit from telling the truth. The Bible says, "you shall know the truth and the truth will set you free" (John 8:32). Renovating your mind involves taking a sober look at yourself and the decisions that have shaped your life. Since life and lifestyle are the result of your decisions, are they based on truth or what is perceived to be true?

Truth vs. The Lie

Admittedly, there is a fine line between what is true and what is not. As God's creation we are not called to straddle that line. Jesus makes it very clear, by the life He lived and the examples He set, that we can't play both sides. Either we're on one side or the other. Which means in order to live a life of truth you must know what the opposing untruths look, feel, taste, and smell like. If fact, to live in God's truth you should even readily depend solely on your natural senses.

People typically pattern their lives after what they perceive to be true. There is a prevailing idea that if an idea or principle can stand the test of time it's true. This line of thought is not necessarily true because it is possible to live in ignorance to truth. Equally possible is the ability to live in stubbornness and rigidity; conforming to what is the norm and comfortable. Take for instance a long-standing untruth many people adopt. Millions of Christians believe that an intimate relationship with Jesus Christ is not necessary. They believe that as long as they don't commit any ghastly crimes, indulge in any serious sin, or physically harm another person they're okay and Heaven bound.

This couldn't be farther from the truth. First, there is no difference between small sin and big sin. There is no "sin scale" to measure ourselves on. Sin is sin. Deception, even self-deception is wrong. Unfortunately society, and to some extent the Church, have categorized sin and placed it on a human-devised scale based on its difficulty or severity. According to worldly standards, lying and deception aren't serious infractions. In reality, a person's ability to operate in deception runs parallel to their ability to sin.

Second, we have all sinned and in some way missed the mark. However, redemption and restoration are available to those who earnestly repent and subscribe to a truth-filled life under the guidance of the Holy Spirit.

Have you ever wondered why people lie to themselves? I've found that the following five reasons are strikingly prominent.

- Embarrassment from past experiences
- To cover up unrighteousness
- To justify a lifestyle they know is not pleasing to God
- Fear of the unknown
- Lack of revelation

Embarrassment From Past Experiences

Your past can sting terribly if you allow it to. I don't know of many born-again believers who are overwhelmingly proud of their pre-salvation years. The whole purpose of salvation through Christ is to cancel behavior-induced bondage and position you for God's promises and purpose. My personal journey through mental renovation was filled with challenges that built my faith. Today I am stronger in God than I have ever been. Still, my past is sometimes difficult to deal with because satan is an expert at issuing condemnation. He consistently keeps his finger on the replay button that leads your old self. He holds old, outdated images, circumstances, and outcomes over your head. Satan knows that if you focus more on the past than God's future, he can cause you to miss on much of God's plan for your life. 2 Corinthians 5: 17 says:

> Therefore if any man be in Christ, he is a new creature: old things are passed away; behold, all things are become new. (KJV)

Dealing With the Past

My mental renovation revealed that I need deliverance from a deeply rooted fear of failure. Benjamin Mays once said, "Not failure, but low aim is sin." My mind was constantly littered with jeering thoughts of past mistakes. It seemed as if the mental torment had taken up permanent residence in my thought life. Once an extremely product-driven person, I put more weight on what was produced rather than how it was produced. In the end if the product wasn't desirable I immediately disregarded any valuable experiences associated with the process. I constantly lied to myself by saying, "maybe if I had tried harder, things would have been better," or "I'm not good enough to make a difference."

Even as I grew up in God, I felt ashamed of my past fears,

associations, and actions. Just a few years ago I could have been the poster child of deception. I was an expert at not allowing my outward appearance to reflect my inner torment. People would ask me, "How are you doing?" Programmed into my reaction was the lie-filled response, "I'm fine." I really wasn't fine. I was lost, in need of a touch from God, but too scared and prideful to ask for it. I was of two opinions. I knew I needed to change, but maintained a well-refined façade that suggested I was fine. My double-mindedness was fueled by empty admiration from others, praise I assumed would add value to who I was. All the while Jesus, the only one who could add value to me, waited patiently for my desperate cry. When I finally humbled myself and cried out for God I sounded similar to David in Psalm 5: 1-7.

> O Lord, hear me as I pray; pay attention to my groaning. Listen to my cry for help, my King and my God, for I pray to no one but you. Listen to my voice in the morning, Lord. each morning I bring my requests to you and wait expectantly. O God, you take no pleasure in wickedness; you cannot tolerate the sins of the wicked. Therefore, the proud may not stand in your presence, for you hate all who do evil. You will destroy those who tell lies. The Lord detests murderers and deceivers. Because of your unfailing love, I can enter your house; I will worship at your Temple with deepest awe.

The Purpose of Your Past

Your past has actually worked and is presently working out for your future good. Adam's failure to accomplish God's desired purpose for him in the garden of Eden means we all must experience difficulty. Our fallen state makes provision for our faith to grow amidst the strenuous of life. Difficulties are God's means of tuning up our lives and strengthening our faith. Another thing our fallen state dictates is the need for a redeemer. Our Redeemer Jesus Christ is the Good News we've been waiting for. And that life-changing news is our sufferings always have a time limit. The transition from mental bondage created by sin to freedom in Christ occurs when you agree with what God has already said about you.

But in that coming day, no weapon turned against you will succeed. And everyone who tells lies in court will be brought to justice. These benefits are enjoyed by the servants of the Lord; their vindication will come from me. I, the Lord, have spoken (Isaiah 54:17 NLT).

For whatsoever is born of God overcometh the world: and this is the victory that overcometh the world, even our faith (1 John 5:4 KJV).

"Do not be afraid of them," the Lord said to Joshua, "for I have given you victory over them. Not a single one of them will be able to stand up to you" (Joshua 10:8 NLT).

You have given me your shield of victory. Your right hand supports me; your help has made me great (Psalm 18:35 NLT).

What God speaks defines. What he says always sets the precedent. At the beginning of the world as we know it God spoke numerous things into existence. What he spoke to had to look like what he said it should look like. God's creation doesn't have the authority to present itself different than what he has spoken. The only thing God used to bring creation into being was time, and with it he accomplished a great deal.

Time: One of His Greatest Tools

It takes time to create. It takes more time to restore. God

29

spent centuries getting His people ready for their Savior. He used kings, prophets, judges, enemies, foes, war, the just, and the corrupt to get His beloved in position to receive His only Son. In these latter times God is up to the task of restoring your life to His intentions by renovating the way you think. He is using men and women anointed and instructed by His Spirit to ready Christians for Christ's return.

Your past is only a point of reference. Any embarrassment or guilt you embrace is not of God because there is no condemnation to those who are in Jesus Christ. As long as you desire the forgiveness of God and intimacy with Christ your past humiliation is rendered powerless. It can no longer shroud your life with regret. When you realize that God has caused you to triumph over past experiences you then commence your Spirit-led journey into God's love and acceptance.

chapter three
surveying the strategy

But don't begin until you count the cost. For who would begin construction of a building without first calculating the cost to see to if there is enough money to finish it? Luke 14:28

Every successful renovation begins with a plan of action.

Inaccurate Interpretation

Satan prides himself on his varied attempts to initiate inaccurate interpretation of God's Word. The devil knows God's Word too. Remember, he was once an angel in heaven, so he recognizes how things work there as well as God's requirements of you. Satan does a good job of presenting the believer with one too many options. All of satan's options are irrelevant and end in disaster. None of his options result in a victorious life for you. Because of this, Jesus admonishes us in Matthew 7:15-16 to:

Beware of false prophets, which come to you in sheep's clothing, but inwardly they are ravening wolves. Ye shall know them by their fruits...(KJV)

As believers we have a duty to ourselves and those we love to be keen observers, not judges, of those who feed us the Word of God. Those who lead us are expected to live upright and blameless lives. There is a marked difference between being self-righteous and being righteous in God. "There is a way which seemeth right unto a man, but the end thereof are the ways of death" (Proverbs 14:12). So, it is absolutely crucial, if the best renovation possible is the goal, for you to submit, if you don't currently, to a pastor whose ministry is based solely on God's Word. I am convinced more than ever that the local church is fertile ground to receive a new level of revelation and power from God through His Spirit. Find a local assembly, led by a leader who displays integrity and character, and a shepherd's heart. A true shepherd always resembles the Good Shepherd. Get planted in a ministry where the Bible is taught and God-ordained friendships and alliances can be nurtured. Remain planted, even during personal difficulty, and watch the fruit of righteousness begin to bloom in your life to the glory of God.

From God's Mouth To Your Mind

Scripture uses the term *dream* to describe how God communicated with many Biblical personalities. Dreams are often vehicles of God's revelation to us, which suggests our need for a better knowledge of His will. Dreams are "gap-fillers" given to   bring clarity to a greater, fuller revelation of God's way of doing things.

The Hebrew word for dream is *chalom* which means to dream while sleeping or to receive, during the course of the dream, prophetic meaning. God, by His Spirit, wants to reveal much about Himself. We see a great example of this in Genesis 20:3 when God spoke to Abimelech in a dream about his dealings with a married woman. Reading the passage you'll discover that Abraham lied about Sarah by telling Abimelech that she was his sister. Abimelech nearly escaped serious trouble because he almost "knew" or had sexual relations with Sarah. God kept Abimelech from sinning because he was truly deceived and therefore innocent. The condition for Abimelech's restoration was that he return to Abraham and receive his prayers. Abraham prayed to God, Abimelech was healed.

Have you possibly missed hearing God because of your state of mind? Often our minds are clouded and cluttered with fascinations, obsessions, and desires that have no positive bearing on our identity or destiny. Studies show that unhappy, hateful people are prone to have more awkward dreams than those whose minds are at peace in God. Can you hear from God during a nightmare? Yes, but nightmares are not a preferred method of communication! They are often warnings or signs that radical change is necessary.

God-ordained dreams are powerful and He may allow you to share them with those in need of direction and clarity for their own situation. Because it is possible to hear God intellectually or spiritually He is seeking spiritual hearers *and* doers. It can be easy, if our focus is not on God, to hear and adhere to wrong teaching more rooted in the will or opinion of a man than of the Master.

The Trap of Tradition Without Truth

A major cause of mental setback among believers is tradition not rooted in truth. Many churches today are not operating at their true potential because they have elected to be comfortable-to be complacent and revel in accomplishments of the past. Nationwide, attendance in weekly worship services has declined drastically. It seems as if many Christian ministries have become reactive instead of proactive. Generations X, Y, and the Millennials are usually not receptive to old methods and antiquated practices.

The foundations of Christian faith must always remain the same, however, the methods we use to reach the lost must adapt to reach a more modern, technologically connected culture. There must be a conscious, well-planned blending of old and new to advance God's causes in this day and time. It is okay to hold to core doctrines and beliefs while exploring new and exciting ways to express those timeless truths.

Distortion of the Worst Kind

Satan tries desperately to distort, or even cancel out, God's revelation to us. God's revelation is His disclosure of divine truth meant to produce a life of freedom and trust in Jesus Christ. One means believers can receive this revelation from God is through dreams and visions. If satan is allowed to pervert the mind, then it can't be used as a receptor of divine information from God. Satan is a subtle and smooth businessman. He'll try to make you an offer you seemingly can't refuse. The truth of the matter is that God's offer is far more rewarding. Accepting God's bid, which He already made through the sacrifice of Jesus Christ on the cross, avails you to a peace and power that defies rational understanding. Christ is the pillar that holds our minds stable for the work of God.

In Song of Solomon 2: 10-15 we get a glimpse of Christ's bride, the church, and the intimate conversation God has with His creation. We battle satan in our minds because we often refuse to acknowledge the seasons of our lives. Let's face truth. If we are not careful, it can become easy to wedge ourselves in a rut of self-denial and deceit. As you proceed through your renovation process, you gain the necessary victorious mentality by acknowledging and accepting the seasons of your life and the authority that God is exercising to your benefit. God's timing is everything.

Song of Solomon 2: 10-15 reveals two commands. First, we are to *arise* and secondly we are to *appear*. It's time to confidently tear down any and all mental strongholds. God didn't create us to be bound; to live with satanic restrictions and boundaries. You and I were created to be free. Jesus came to set us free, so why be bound? If we have to be bound by something, let it be God's love, righteousness, holiness, and glory.

In Galatians 5:1 we also find more instructions from God. We are commanded to "Stand fast therefore in the liberty wherewith Christ hath made us free, and be not entangled again with the yoke of bondage." The renovation of the mind leads to freedom from deception, doubt, fear, greed, guilt, heaviness, jealousy, legalism, resentment, restlessness, sexual idolatry, self-centeredness, shame, unbelief, worldliness, perfectionism, frustration, depression, additions, and complaining-just to name a few. Be free in Jesus' name!

Even during the season of demolition, God desires that you be steadfast and unmovable. You might ask, "How am I to arise when everything around me is crumbling?" The answer lies in the fact that God has promised His protection. You will not dash your foot against a stone (Psalm 91:12) because He has given angels charge over you. That means that He takes care of us. No harm will come up upon us. We will not fall. God's angels have your back. The demolition process is not designed to kill you. It's intended by God to build strength and create focus. Why? God is preparing you for the next level of purpose and it's associated blessings.

Arise, God's People

No doubt, arising can be tough. I often experience difficulty rising from bed after a night's rest. My mind says "get up and get your day started" but, my body says "no, I'm staying in bed." According the original biblical terminology, arising suggests being strong with purpose. In Greek the term is *anatello,* which literally means to *spring up* or *rise from.*

The time has come for God's people to spring up from mental turmoil and instability. Some churches suffer because leadership and/or membership are ill-equipped to dominate the enemy in mental spiritual warfare. There are pastors who only preach to entertain, not to see people transformed. The Gospel is too often sugarcoated, pacified, and relegated to the support human agenda. People can't "spring up" for being held down by teaching and preaching that doesn't point to Jesus Christ.

Returning to Song of Solomon 2: 10-15, after we arise we must then appear. By appear I don't just imply the act of showing up. In this context the word *appear* denotes to *show forth.* People are not going to always believe in the God we talk about, they will believe the God we cause them to see.

Eradicating the Old Mindset

People in covenant with God, possess the power through Jesus by the Holy Spirit to make positive changes to their life. For years I was bound by a negative self-image. Incapable of genuine love or friendship, I trusted no one. I decided to only look out for myself. By maintaining that selfish mindset I only burrowed a deeper hole of disappointment and despair. I memorialized my hopes, dreams, and aspirations. Instead of burying hate, lust, and depression, I eulogized love, positive thinking, trust, healthy relationships, and my dependency on God. However, after great anguish sobering from scripture and counseling, I made a conscious decision to allow my mind to be renovated from the ground up. Before the process could truly begin I knew some demolition work had to be done. For me it all began with a simple prayer through song:

Change me,
Into Your image Lord,
Into Your likeness Lord,
Change me

I want to be like You,
Be like You,
Oh Lord,
Change me!

My life changed forever after singing this simple worship chorus at a leadership conference. I felt the presence of the Lord. As I wept in repentance, I experienced God's forgiveness and restoration. With eyes shut and heart wide open I accepted God's will for my life and stepped into His love, power, and assurance. Immediately I was hungry to receive accurate interpretation of the Bible. I knew I needed to experience the power of God's Word so that I would be equipped to help others discover and walk out their purpose and destiny.

God always has a plan. His strategy for the genesis of my mental renovation was excellently executed. I was in the right place at the right time. As you survey the strategy in consultation with the Holy Spirit, keep an open mind and heart. Remember God has a plan of action to achieve His ultimate goal in you. Because renovating the mind doesn't happen without opposition, allow God to plan and direct the operation of your mind in this aspect of spiritual warfare. Victory is assured. Freedom is imminent. The best life possible is extremely attainable.

chapter four
God is in your mess

Blessing God and building up others, thrusts us into a position of favor and influence. This position creates the opportunity for God to work in and through us to effect change in countless lives. However, serving God is not the easiest thing to do. Accepting God's mandate of mental renovation comes with a price. It takes obedience and sacrifice.

Serving is a journey. There will be hills to climb and rivers to cross. Climbing hills takes energy and stamina. Crossing rivers takes the willingness to get a little wet. Times will come when you want to throw in the towel and do something else. At times, when serving God, everything else looks so much better. Everything else looks so easy.

It's easy for a tired, burned-out, used, abused servant of God to slip though the cracks back to a life of sin and destruction. I've seen it happen many times. The fed up believer eventually says, "God, you didn't say I had to go through all of this mess." After a season of mental exhaustion and disappointment because things didn't go the way they expected the proverbial question is asked, "God, where are you?"

Seeking Clarity

As clarity is sought, God simply says, "I was there all along and I'm here now." God tells us in Deuteronomy 31:8 that the He goes before us and would never forsake us. We have no reason to be afraid and discouraged. God allows difficult situations to strengthen our relationship with Him. Personally, I have learned some of my most poignant lessons about life and love during extremely difficult seasons. It was in those times that I came to lean and depend on God more than ever. When no one else is available to help, God is always ready to step in. The more we depend on Him, the more we come to know Him.

At His Name

When of the opinion that all is hopeless and no options remain, call on the name of Jesus. At the mention of His name, every knee must bow and every tongue has no choice but to confess that Jesus is Lord. Even satan has to yield to God. Isn't it reassuring to know that demons tremble when you call on the name of your Lord and Savior? Clarity becomes a reality when we apply faith in Jesus Christ through His name.

Jesus is Lord and Savior. He is all the world anyone who confesses with their mouth and believes in their heart that He was born of the Virgin Mary, died on Calvary's cross, and arose to be seated in Heaven with His Father. We have a mighty strong friend, a worthy confidant. The elderly ladies of a church I once served still sing the following hymn today during devotion time:

What a friend we have in Jesus,
All our sins and grieves to bear,
What a privilege to carry,

Everything to God in prayer.

Thrive Through It

You may not believe it, but God is right in the midst of your mess. He's omnipresent; everywhere at the same time. Not one detail of what happens on earth escapes His sight. His desire is that we thrive through every adverse situation. The word *thrive* means to grow or develop well. *Thrive* also means to flourish and prosper.

In difficult times what else is there to do? Calling on the name of Jesus is but one way to get God attention. Thriving through any situation also involves rehearsing victories, praying, speaking and living out God's word, and being patient. Three of the four ways to thrive are related to the Word of God. This is because Scripture was inspired and given by God to be the ultimate instruction manual for humans. Just as a new VCR or stereo comes with an instruction manual, so do we.

Follow the Instructions

An analogy I often draw about the Word of God likens it to assembling a piece of furniture. A while ago, a friend and I undertook the task of assembling a large entertainment center for his family room. The box was massive, accurately indicating how expansive the project would be. While unpacking the box, we noticed that all pieces of wood were labeled. This proved beneficial as we began the process. During the course of assembling that monstrosity, we must have referred to the instructions a hundred times. And, even though we followed the instructions as carefully as possible—we still made a couple of mistakes. Some mistakes we fixed, but others were beyond our repair; like the chipped section on the back. Yep, we hid that one well. After about two hours, we completed the entertainment center. My friend then turned to his wife and sighed, "Never again!"

God's Word was created to address our specific needs. It comforts or confronts, depending on our relationship with God or the presence of sin in our life. After hearing and receiving what God is saying, it is up to us to place our faith Him. A rewarding life is built and patterned after the precepts of God's Word. To others it may look as if you're in a million pieces-broken to the point of no return. People might not understand the internal work God is performing until He has completed your mental renovation. Don't worry about what people think or say. Stay focused on what God is accomplishing during this process. There will be signs of progress posted along the way. I know first-hand that signs like increased joy, renewed focus, and ramped-up faith will be evident. It's up to those around you whether or not they take time to read and accurately interpret those signs. Hopefully those signs of God's work will lead others to realize their need for mental renovation also.

Partner with the Holy Spirit to reconstruct your life God's way. God's Spirit knows your instruction manual, the Bible, completely. He inspired the writers to write everything contained in it. The more you know God's Word, the more you'll be able to recognize the victories you've already won and the ones you will win in the future.

Rehearse Your Victories

At this point you should know what part of the body satan attacks the most. He loves to attack the mind. Satan expends an enormous amount of energy attempting to pollute every mind he can gain access to. If access is granted, satan will definitely not pass up the opportunity to destroy a person's faith, hope, love, and respect for God. If the devil can change the way a person thinks, he can change the person. If he can change the person, he can change who that person influences. The effect can go on an on if it's not addressed aggressively. Since what we think shapes our lives, it is important that our thoughts operate in the direction we want to go. Proverbs 23: 7 says that whatsoever a man thinketh in his heart, so is he.

The enemy wants the mind think about things his way. He wants you to adopt his philosophy about you. Satan desires to brainwash, confuse, dismantle, and utterly destroy God's plan and course of action. One way the devil gets the upper hand is by confusing the mind. James 3: 15-17 speaks well about confusion and what causes it.

> This wisdom descendeth not from above, but is earthly, sensual, devilish. For where envying and strife is, there is confusion and every evil work. But the wisdom that is from above is first pure, then peaceable, gentle, and easy to be intreated, full of mercy and good fruits, without partiality, and without hypocrisy (James 3:15-17 KJV).

To rehearse victories, there must first be order in the mind. Therefore, a renovation of the mind is extremely necessary. A clouded mind is the devil's playground. Confusion kills. It kills marriages, friendships, opportunities, and success. It kills hope, joy, and even communication. As Children of God it is vitally important for us to seek and speak clarity to our minds and hearts. The wisdom referred to in James 3:15 is not wisdom from the Almighty. It is earthly, sensual and devilish. We know that those adjectives in no way describe anything our Lord is.

> But if you are bitterly jealous and there is selfish ambition in your heart, don't cover up the truth with boasting and lying. For jealousy and selfishness are not God's kind of wisdom. Such things are earthly, unspiritual, and demonic. For wherever there is jealousy and selfish ambition, there you will find disorder and evil of every kind (James 3: 14).

The Word of God states over and over again that we are victorious. In fact, if you flip to the end of the Bible, you'll discover that we win! There is absolutely nothing the devil can do to prevent our victory. Victory comes through none other than Jesus Christ. Rehearsing victories involves making a decision to see the good as good and the bad as good also.

Seeing Good As Good

> Whatever is good and perfect comes down to us from God our Father, who created all the lights in the heavens. He never changes or casts a shifting shadow (James 1:17).

God is the author of every acceptable, pleasant, agreeable, and joyful gift. He is also is the source of every mature, full-grown, integrity-filled gift. God desires that the good of life be celebrated. If what's wrong about life is over-emphasized we become slaves to negative thoughts and mental imagery. A better, joy-filled life is possible if we rehearse the awesome things God has allowed us to experience. Whether it's the birth of a child, promotion on the job, or conquering a fear, God is worthy to be praised. As you rehearse your victories think about how God has blessed you to be a blessing. Take a moment to think about how good God has been to you and those you love. Celebrating at our high points is easy, but what about when everything is not peaches and cream?

Seeing the Good In the Bad

Everything that happens does so for a reason. Because God never relinquishes control to anyone, all we encounter is monitored by Him. Yes, even the most difficult and uncomfortable circumstances are within God's purview. Look at it this way. Trials are actually training. A *trial* is a person, thing, or situation that tests a person's endurance. We are stretched during seasons of testing. Sometimes going through life is like taking a pop-quiz everyday. It can feel as if you are never prepared for what's next. Even in difficult times God wants to bless you beyond your wildest imagination. Trials come to prepare us for what we're not ready for yet. I refer again to Job's experience with God in the midst of trial. Job walked uprightly before the Lord. He was a man of great substance and was well respected among his family and acquaintances. It looks as if Job had everything he needed-wealth, relationship with God, and a good name. I would liken Job to a well-respected businessman in the community. He's a faithful leader in the church, has a beautiful wife and children. He tithes, gives generous offerings, and volunteers his time and talent for kingdom building.

Despite Job's resume, satan was walking around looking for something or someone to get into and God ends up offering him up. No one said being a righteous believer was going to be a walk in the park. As the story goes, Job experiences numerous hardships; loosing his family, friends, wealth, and even the will to live. Through it all, Job refused to curse God. He refused to wish that evil or misfortune come upon his Maker.

The Book of Job contains forty-two chapters. Job is afflicted for forty-one of them. How can it be that God would cause one of His best to suffer so much? The answer lies in understanding the concept of love. You are one of God's best, however, victory can't be manifested in you until your mind-set has changed. Victorious living is not only about health, wealth, and prosperity. It's also about faith.

I know some very troubled millionaires. They are devoid of peace because their primary concern is making money and how not loose what they already have. They are submerged under years of mental anguish and stress. Smiling in public is but a façade to a deep pain and sorrow. Convinced that victory lies solely in worldly possessions and power, they don't fully trust and depend on God as their Ultimate Source. They haven't learned and adopted the F.R.O.G. principle. F.R.O.G is an acronym for *fully reliant upon God.* If God took all their riches away, would they still follow Him? If God took what you have away for a season, would you still follow Him?

The Others

On the other hand, I have encountered people who were not affluent, who live from paycheck to paycheck, whose bills are often late, who deal with collection agencies on a regular basis, who struggle to make ends meet. Nevertheless, they were at peace with their circumstances. They weren't out of their trials at that moment but they understood that God would give garments of praise for the times when heaviness weighs in. These people live out Isaiah 61: 3.

> To all who mourn in Israel, he will give a crown of beauty for ashes, a joyous blessing instead of mourning, festive praise instead of despair. In their righteousness, they will be like great oaks that the Lord has planted for his own glory.

Job had awesome faith in God and he put it to work. In Chapter 42 we see that because Job spoke truth about God, interceded for his friends, he is rewarded handsomely for his patience and endurance. Job is a firm example of real faith.

> And the Lord turned the captivity of Job, when he prayed for his friends: also the Lord gave Job twice as much as he had before (Job 42:10 KJV).

Strive to become affluent in the Fruits of the Spirit – love, joy, peace, forbearance, kindness, goodness, faithfulness, gentleness, and self-control. If you do that, God will definitely take care of everything else.

chapter five
emancipation from fear

Generally, when the word *emancipation* is mentioned, our thinking hovers around the liberation of a nation or large group of people. However, it can be applied in usage to our personal lives as well. To *emancipate* basically means to free from restraint. That's exactly what Jesus Christ accomplished for us by dying on the cross. We were forever released from the bondage placed upon us by sin. Sin only possesses the power we give it. As a result of consistent unhealthy decisions, based on ungodly thoughts, sin became a vice. But in God's Word we discover what Jesus accomplished for all who believe in Him. Galatians 5: 1 makes it clear that we have been made free by Christ and should by all means remain free.

Exposing Fear

Fear is a learned behavior. A well-known acronym for *fear* is *false evidence appearing real*. It is typically produced from a combination of observation and direct personal experience. For example, people tend to develop fear because of what they have seen. Fear though observation is a terrible trick of the enemy and must be proactively addressed if we plan to maintain a victorious mindset. Millions, maybe billions of people fail to set goals because of the failure they have seen or heard about. Fear grows when curiosity and doubt are allowed to mingle. Fear seeks to destroy inspiration, disrupt innovation, and to eventually cause stagnation. It manifests itself as the voice within that speaks against destiny and God-given authority. It says that what everyone else has experienced will be your story. If it happened to them, it's going to happen to you. Fear says crazy things like, "Since my mother died young, I'm going to die young too." Or, "Because my father died of cancer, that's how I'm doing to die too." Fear perpetuates the lie that you won't, you can't, nor will you ever achieve God's best for your life.

Everyone else's circumstance is not necessarily your circumstance. God could be waiting on you be bold and to try something new and different. God might say, "Start that business, seek that promotion, finish that college degree, pursue that goal." Or he might even say, "Leave that person alone." If God asks you to leave something or someone alone, it's always for good reason. Fear says the opposite of everything God says. When God says, "You can," fear says, "Oh no you can't."

Fear is an unpleasant emotion caused by the anticipation or awareness of danger. It is a strong emotion that seeks to paralyze the thought process, thereby severely impairing the ability to make sound, faith-based, God-pleasing decisions. It's satan's attempt to stagnate progress toward the success God has destined for us. Fear is not the product of the Holy Spirit within you. The Spirit of God within you doesn't cohabitate nor cooperate with fear. It is antithetical to fear because 2 Timothy 1: 7 says that, "God hath not given us the spirit of fear; but of power, and of love, and of a sound mind."

Fear is actually a perversion of the spirit of expectation. Thoughts are invaded with doubt and suspicion. Expectation is very important to anyone who has desires and aspirations.

The spirit of expectation is birthed from an unshakable conviction that God has and never will fail at keeping His promise to provide, protect, and nurture us. Someone who understands the power of expectation knows that goodness and mercy with follow them all the days of their life (Psalm 23:6). Also, people with great expectations know what fear can do to faith. Fear tolerated equals faith contaminated.

I'll Have No Part of It

One of the biggest indicators of a fear-filled mindset is avoidance behavior. This type of behavior eventually leads to a lack of self-discipline. Fearful people engage in things that avoid feelings and emotions associated with discomfort. Instead of participating in what God desires, they settle for whatever causes the least amount of resistance or difficulty.

Avoidance behavior looks like this. Sam schedules an appointment with his physician but cancels it at the last possible moment because he fears needles. Sam sabotaged his appointment even though the injections contained medicine of great benefit to him. Sam's fear doesn't lie in the possibility of getting well. His problem is in the process necessary to see results. So, Sam struggles through additional pain and anguish despite help being available. He has subscribed himself to doing it his way. Health and prosperity are the products of a life filled with processes that build character and faith.

A person who employs avoidance behavior to disengage from God's purposes for their life is actually disconnecting themselves from His will.

Expect God To Do It

A believer's expectation that all things work for their good is intrinsically linked to the manifestation of God's will. When we are connected to God's will we can expect His divine assistance and assurance. Without God there is not much worth expecting, much less hoping for.

To expect something means that you look forward to it. Hope is birthed from expectation. God expects us to wake up every morning expecting Him to do something spectacular in and through us. The devil also wants us to expect. He wants us to expect that nothing good will happen to us on any given day. Since satan is the Father of Lies (John 8: 44) we have the authority through Jesus Christ to void out what he desires and instead train our minds to reflect and expect what God wants. Therefore, during your mental renovation, one chief aim should be to eradicate the fear of failure.

The Fear of Failure

The fear of failure is prevalent in our modern culture. Like me, you have probably experienced the fear of potentially failing as a parent, spouse, in your career, or even as a Christian. For me, the fear of failure caused unnecessary dread, apprehension, stress, and pain. Because I was afraid of failure, and the ridicule that might follow, I didn't attempt many things as an adolescent. Since I defined myself by what others thought and assumed, I had a terribly difficult time discovering my worth as an individual. For me back then, a healthy self-image was almost non-existent. My fears eventually led to severe avoidance behavior, which caused me to abstain from participating in anything that would reveal the gifts God had placed inside me. As a result, I missed out on many opportunities to represent God and give Him glory. As I reflect back, now through the lenses of my God-defined worth, I observe that much of the rejection I experienced occurred in the context of the church. As rejection built a fortress around my heart, I slowly developed a distrust of anyone who claimed to represent God. I applied that line of thinking to everyone, from the front door to the pulpit. Deep down I knew I wasn't being who God created me to be. I was hungry for more of God but didn't know how to proceed by His mercy and through His grace. I was at point of desperation. Something had to change-and something did.

Pursuit Equals Turnaround

The turnaround began when I chose to pursue God's approval instead of those around me. In essence, I had to kick one of the main manifestations of the fear of failure to the curb-people bondage. God healed me of the hurt I sustained in the church. I then decided that if I was going to fail anymore that I would fail forward. At least I would fall closer to my goal; learning everything I could from the experience. It is a tragedy to fall backward. The last thing anyone might desire is to fall backward into their past and be entrapped by it.

David, the anointed and appointed leader of Israel, said in Psalm 34: 4-6, 10.

> I sought the Lord, and he answered me and delivered me from all my fears. Those who look to him are radiant, and their faces shall never be ashamed....The young lions suffer want and hunger, but those who seek the Lord lack no good thing (ESV).

It seems as if opportunities constantly abound to halt forward momentum toward God and revert back to old ways of thinking and doing. These devil-inspired opportunities for regression are usually presented through un-renovated thoughts about failure, disappointment, discouragement, or even selfish success, which eventually breed pride and contempt for others. The devil wants nothing more than for your past to prevent your glorious future from materializing. Even more than that, the devil is terrified that the promises of God for your future will actually come to pass through God's providential power.

In contrast to satan, God has greatness in store for you. Satan's strategy is to convince you that your past days are the best you'll ever have. The plan is to get you to negate your future in God, cause you to dwell in the land of complacency, and be locked away in a hopeless cycle of sin and distrust of God.

In the Bible, Paul reminds the Galatian Church of the freedom they qualified for through the blood of Jesus Christ. In Galatians 5: 13 he says,

> For you have been called to live in freedom, my brothers and sisters. But don't use your freedom to satisfy your sinful nature. Instead, use your freedom to serve one another in love.

We don't qualify for the freedom Paul is referring to because of anything we've done. It's a free gift of grace that flows into our lives because of Christ's sacrifice. Ephesians 2: 8-9 says,

> God saved you by his grace when you believed. And you can't take credit for this; it is a gift from God. Salvation is not a reward for the good things we have done, so none of us can boast about it.

We have been given an awesome gift to be used to bless others. We accomplish Christ's motives and purposes through the spirit of love. Love is the foundation upon which God desires to build the lives of His most treasured possession-all mankind.

True freedom has its foundation in love. The God-kind-of-love is not based on circumstance, but upon a loving Father who desires only the best for His children. While we were still in sin, God loved us with a deep, passionate, sin-defying love--a love that conquered all fear and doubt. God's love is eternal. This God-kind-of-love knows no equal. It's a love that transcends space and time and redeems us into an intimate dependence on our Maker and Lord. God's love is eternal, everlasting, and definitely conquers all.

True Freedom

True freedom rooted in love also leads to true dependence on Jesus Christ. At first, it may seem like a conflict to be free yet dependent on someone else. The last thing anyone wants to feel is vulnerable, because our culture's definition of dependence leans toward that. We experience emancipation from our old ways, habits, thoughts, dispositions, fears, and attitudes when we pick up the love of Christ and intentionally depend on Him to mature it in us. When you integrate God's concept of intentional love into your thought life bitterness, pain, discouragement, and other mental ills can't keep up. A renovated mind truly accepts that love conquers all. Healing and deliverance are merely by-products of a heart and mind that is content with loving others as Christ loved and is still loving us.

I know, all this seems a bit lofty, especially when a love-less culture seems to be prevalent, but with God all things are possible. You can't accomplish mental emancipation on your own. You won't realize victory over the demons of an un-renovated mind because of your individual strength or wit. It will happen only by the hand of God in cooperation with your will and desire. If you are willing and obedient, freedom is available and yours for the taking.

Freedom Means...

It's an awesome feeling to be free. Freedom definitely has its benefits, but also has inherent responsibilities associated with it. Freedom in Christ is the catalyst of the freedom we

experience in our everyday lives. Freedom in its spiritual con-
notation can be defined as *exemption from liability.* If it was not
for Christ's unselfish sacrifice on our behalf, we would be liable
for every wrong thought and action. God, in His graciousness,
exempted us from eternal pain and suffering through the blood
of Jesus Christ. This exemption, issued by God, is our ultimate reason to think like God wants us to think. We are loved
and cherished. Moreover, our freedom is a reminder that our
thoughts should consistently hold God in high regard. Proverbs 1: 7 reminds us that the fear of the Lord is the beginning of knowledge. Centering your thoughts on God allows
the mind to receive knowledge correctly—via revelation from
His Word.

That's why you must align your thinking with the fact
that you have an advocate, friend, brother, confidant, teacher,
encourager, advisor, and leader who loves you with a passionate expression of Himself. To be free is to realize that sinful
thoughts and their corresponding actions no longer have the
power to dominate your life. God has given us authority to
cast down every diabolical scheme that attempts to discredit
us. The freedom to exercise the power of love is ours so that
God's Kingdom may be advanced in the earth. You were created to operate without the constraints that fear levies upon
you. A renovated mind is a free mind. To borrow the words of
the songwriting duo McElroy and Foster, "free your mind and
the rest will follow." Maybe a better rendering would be "allow
God to free your mind and the *best* will follow!"

chapter six
real faith

"Faith, like light, should always be simple and unbending; while love, like warmth, should beam forth on every side, and bend to every necessity of our brethren." - Martin Luther

How real is your faith? Any faith worth having is faith worth using. Do you believe God's Word with your whole heart? Does what God say govern the way you act, think, and perceive? During mental renovation a God kind-of-faith must be developed. God has dealt each of us a tailor-made amount of faith to execute His will here on earth. A God kind-of-faith isn't solely based on faith in people and temporal things. It's rooted in things eternal and purposed by the sovereignty of God. The crux of faith involves unwavering trust. This trust boils down to believing God even when visual evidence says otherwise. Faith accepts God as the absolute authority on life. It takes faith to live well. God is the General Contractor on any mental renovation project. He holds all permits so all reconstruction can happen in an orderly and timely manner.

It Hurts For Our Good

God allows circumstances into our lives for a divine reason. Trials and adversity are part and parcel of training God has designed to propel us to the next level of life. The hold up for many people is their desire to achieve the next level, but by doing it their way. If God allowed us to run our lives with no input from Him, we would self-destruct. Living a life of faith involves developing a growing sense of God's guidance. God opens doors to us—especially doors we hadn't expected to be opened. When those doors are discovered that's when our faith must be enacted. Successfully navigating unknown territory takes faith based in intimacy with God.

As we willingly participate in mental transformation, God's promises, which are His opened doors to favor, health, prosperity, and eternal life through Jesus Christ, become clearer. There is assurance in Numbers 23:19:

> God is not a man, so he does not lie. He is not human, so he does not change his mind. Has he ever spoken and failed to act? Has he ever promised and not carried it through?

What God Is Not

Faith in God's promises has the power keep you going even when the journey seems unbearable. When in trouble many people rehearse in their minds what God is. We know that He is a keeper, healer, watchman, shelter, and so many other things in hard times. But, in times of adversity I also find comfort in what God is not. There are very few passages in the Bible that begin with "God is not." When mentioned, the phrase refers to God not being in a place or with a group of people. However, let's focus on the phrase in the context of God's attributes.

I am the God of Abraham, and the God of Isaac, and the

God of Jacob? God is not the God of the dead, but of the living. Matthew 22:32 (KJV)

For God is not the author of confusion, but of peace, as in all churches of the saints (1 Corinthians 14:33 KJV).

For God is not unrighteous to forget your work and labour of love, which ye have shewed toward his name, in that ye have ministered to the saints, and do minister (Hebrews 6:10 KJV).

But now they desire a better country, that is, a heavenly: wherefore God is not ashamed to be called their God: for he hath prepared for them a city (Hebrews 11:16 KJV).

Of course, we know that God is not anything evil. From the verses above we discover that God is not:

- The God of the dead, but the living
- The author of confusion, but of peace
- Unrighteous
- Ashamed

There is great comfort in knowing what God is and is not. Now let's turn our attention to a few things God is.

God of the Living

A mind that has not been renovated or renewed is a dying mind. God desires to be Lord and Lover of every aspect of us, including our mind. People fall by the wayside everyday because they refuse to allow God to be their guide. James 1:8 states that "A double minded man is unstable in all his ways." Living a life that pleases God takes concentrated effort. We know this because the Apostle Paul says in Romans 7:21 that "when I would do good, evil is present with me." Paul, even as powerful vessel of God, at times struggled to live a life that pleased God. Evil will always attempt to present itself as a viable option to what is good as pleasing to God.

The purpose of mental renovation is to remove the old and irrelevant and replace it with the new and relevant. In a way we allow God to reinvest Himself in us. The more room God occupies within us the less room there is for anything else. Sometimes we need renovation from the ground up.

During a typical renovation the foundation usually remains while everything that challenges the structural integrity of the building must be replaced. What looks excellent on the outside could be damaged and unstable on the inside. I have toured many potential investment properties that on the surface looked worth time and effort. Excitement was a common emotion as I dreamt about the possibilities for monetary gain from the property. In a few instances, after thorough inspection, several structural inconsistencies were found that did not justify investment. Thank God I took the time to investigate what lurked behind outward cosmetic beauty. Thorough analysis saved me money and unnecessary distress.

Likewise, God does thorough assessments. God has decided to invest Himself in your mental renovation. God wants to restore you from the inside out and cause you to shine among people still in darkness. Jesus put it this way:

> I have come as a light to shine in this dark world, so that all who put their trust in me will no longer remain in the dark. John 12:46.

The God of Peace

God is not the God of confusion. Unfortunately, there

are people who don't know what to believe. Don't compromise your position in God by holding two opinions.

Wherever confusion exists there is always rebellion against God's will. In many contexts confusion implies revolution or anarchy. The spirit of confusion mounts itself against the work of the Kingdom of God. People who operate within the confines of confusion often lose track of God's presence in their lives. They begin to question the very existence of God and His power. Confused people are distraught, hurt, and usually look for answers in all the wrong places.

The enemy will attempt to confuse you during the renovation process by painting pictures that are not a part of God's purposeful masterpiece for your life. They are pictures not portraits. The devil wants you to believe that what is now will always be the case.

Portraits Not Pictures

Satan's pictures are not portraits. What is the difference between a portrait and a picture? Let me explain metaphorically.

Since the beginning of time God has been planning and promoting His masterpiece. That unique masterpiece is you. God decided when He began the effort that He would not rush. He determined that He would take His time. What we have done, sometimes unknowingly, is step outside of ourselves and attempted to understand what God was creating in us. When we didn't fully comprehend we took it upon ourselves to attempt to correct what God was doing. In essence, through sin, we took our hands and smeared the masterwork before the paint dried. No matter how much you and I smeared the work, God in His grace and mercy quickly erased our mistake with a single color-the crimson blood of Jesus Christ. God performed these corrective measures over and over again because

He is interested in creating and preserving a masterwork that has the power to bless future generations. When the mind is fully renovated we are blessed to be a blessing.

Now, a picture is akin to instant gratification. A portrait takes time to create. There is sweat equity involved. There is a creative thrust that can only occur when the anointing of God is present. Conversely, a picture is developed by a third-party. Even with modern technology and our ability to print pictures at home we still depend on a machine to produce the image. In the Spirit realm that third-party is satan. In the natural many of us lack the skill or equipment to develop our own photographs. Therefore, we take a roll of film or a memory card and entrust it to a photo developer for manifestation. That developer specializes in returning pictures to the owner quickly. It's akin to a quick fix. Satan even goes as far as creating counterfeit pictures of an original masterpiece to lure believers from their God-ordained purpose and process. Beware of imitators. They are the perpetrators of confusion.

God's work on the mind is not a one-hour developmental process. It involves His life-changing power paired with a person's submission to the cause. God takes as long as He deems necessary. He cares so much that He's willing to create your new life on His terms so that you can operate in His glory. Again, Paul quotes God in 2 Corinthians 4: 6:

> For God, who said "Let there be light in darkness," has made this light shine in our hearts so we could know the glory of God that is seen in the face of Jesus Christ.

Peace In The Process

God takes His time with the creation and development of great things. There is no need to rush. His timing is incalculable. A thousand years are like a day to the Lord (2 Peter 3:8).

Remember, He is the creator of all things and He does it all extremely well. Jesus said in John 16:33:

> These things I have spoken unto you, that in me ye might have peace. In the world ye shall have tribulation: but be of good cheer; I have overcome the world.

In Jesus Christ an abundance of peace and patience is available. This peace leads us to love and serve rather than rebel and distract. When in a confused and un-renovated state, we distract others. Notice in the passage above that Jesus assured us that we would have peace and tribulation. Tribulation is where many people fall off the wagon because they lack peace, patience, and perseverance in the process. Blessings are assigned wherever the peace of God abounds. Whenever and wherever tribulation exists, God's peace is abundantly available. Invite the peace of God into your life and reap the benefits associated with it. One of the major benefits of peace is joy.

A Place For Joy To Reside

A renovated mind allows for fullness of joy to reside in a person. That fullness radiates from their life when they recognize Jesus is their Source. We derive strength from the promises found in His Word. When joy is active past, present, or future circumstances have no power to consume our thoughts. We are defined by God, not our situations. Look at the following verses from the Bible:

> The LORD will give strength unto his people; the LORD will bless his people with peace (Psalm 29:11 KJV).

> Mercy and truth are met together; righteousness and peace have kissed each other. Truth shall spring out of the earth; and righteousness shall look down from heaven. Yea, the

> LORD shall give that which is good; and our land shall yield her increase. Righteousness shall go before him; and shall set us in the way of his steps (Psalm 85: 10-13 KJV).

> He maketh peace in thy borders, and filleth thee with the finest of the wheat (Psalm 147:14 KJV).

Simply put, God's peace is attainable when we submit wholeheartedly to the renovation process. Once God begins the process, there emerges the awesome opportunity to revolutionize our thinking, perception, and awareness of our worth to the Kingdom of God.

Because renovating the mind is process-oriented, take note of the experiences that frame the journey. Some people only desire the end product, de-emphasizing or even forsaking the process. We actually receive God's power while in the process. God is interested in us "working out our salvation." He is the Alpha and Omega. He already knows what has, what is, and what will happen. We hit snags when we try to manipulate the process. Satan's biggest weapon against you is you. Embrace the peace that God offers through His Spirit, His Scripture, His shepherds (pastors) and live a more fulfilled existence.

Righteousness and Assurance

God is the ultimate example of righteousness. He is righteous and fair in all He does. We might not understand why, how, or when things happen, but we can depend on God to know what's best for us, even when it doesn't feel good. The not so good is inserted into your life so that God can teach you to trust Him. Deuteronomy 6:25 says:

> For we are righteous when we obey all the commands the LORD our God has given us.

God is the ultimate expression of righteous because He can't contradict himself. He can't disobey Himself. He is the essence of everything we should be. We become righteous when we trust and obey God. A sure sign of an un-renovated mind is disobedience. God has filled the Bible with commands and laws for us to live by. Unfortunately, people ignore these basic statutes to their own demise. Some people know better but refuse to do what they know is right and good. Doing better has its corresponding rewards.

God Is Worth It

God rewards those who obey Him. He enjoys blessing those who walk uprightly before Him. However, our carnal nature is always at war with the Spirit of God within us. A constant tension exists between our earthly, temporal nature and our spiritual connection with God. Nevertheless, like Abraham, righteousness belongs to us because of our obedience. Abraham was called righteous by God because he trusted and obeyed.

The cause of righteousness is as admirable as its effect. Righteousness is caused by a need to experience the fullness of God by adhering yourself to His divine will. The problem lies in the fact that some people are ignorant of their need to know God more. Others just don't desire a closer more profound relationship with God. They have no qualms letting you know that they are "fine where they are." I am convinced that our political, socioeconomic, and familial climates would be healthier and more productive if the development of true relationship with God were more important. Those who are committed to knowing God don't shun the renovation process.

A Great Effect

A major by-product of righteousness is assurance. In Isaiah 31:17 we discover that peace, quietness, and confidence are all products of righteousness. We all can use more peace, quietness, and confidence. Confidence, in this context, is synonymous with assurance. The assurance that we possess is a blessed one. This type of confidence can only come from God's Spirit. Any assurance given by the world's standards is false assurance. It's an assurance that can only be made real through the efforts of our carnal nature. Yes, false assurance can net you results that produce only a temporary, surface-like effect.

Sam is concerned about his job. For the past few weeks his employer has been laying thousands of people off. He decides that he will create some assurance himself by trying to win his boss' favor. To do so he engages in improper acts because that's what he has been told to do in order to secure his position. What Sam doesn't know is that his boss' job is on the chopping block too. Eventually, because Sam trusted in what a supervisor could do for him more than God, he lost his position on the same day as his boss.

God's assurance never leads us to make decisions that displease Him. Having confidence in God's ability to provide is assurance to the max. Things that ultimately determine our direction must be rooted in holiness, righteousness, and faith. Some people have difficulty believing that God's assurance is all we need to live happy and productive lives. Remember, God cannot and will not lie to us. In Genesis 1:3-4 we experience the power of God's spoken Word.

> Then God said, "Let there be light," and there was light. And God saw that the light was good. Ten he separated the light from the darkness.

God's spoken Word is final. God says what He wants and then sees it come to pass. God wanted light and without any hesitation light became a reality. Not only did the light appear but it was good. When God gives you His assurance the result is going to be good. God chose to emphasize how awesome His creative power is by assigning an adjective to what manifested. He does the same when He speaks about His love for us.

> But I lavish unfailing love for a thousand generations on those who love me and obey my commandments (Exodus 20:6).

Based on what He spoke in Genesis 1, God wanted us to inhabit the earth. Therefore, before we were formed in the womb He knew us (Jeremiah 1:5). When you were born God said, "It is good." And yes, you have inhabited the earth. What God spoke in Genesis 1 has definitely come to pass. The evidence is that you're here reading this sentence right now. To God be the glory!

After the manifestation of light occurred, God gave it purpose. He doesn't waste words. After He speaks to you, the objective and purpose is for you to bless others as a result of what you have heard and received. On the other end of the renovation process, toward its completion, is the ability to conceive and believe. People with renovated minds are able to speak things into existence. They speak by faith and eagerly await the manifestation.

Speak what God has spoken about you and where you're headed Then pair your faith with corresponding works to experience the manifestation. Faith without works doesn't work.

A renovated mind is always open to hearing from God for the benefit of others. Your existence is not only about you. That's why God is spending valuable time nudging you, by His Spirit, toward your destiny. Reaching your point of destiny is up to you. So, it is of vital importance that you not fight the process. As I have said, the enemy wants to convince you that the process will kill you. That is the farthest thing from the truth. No matter how long God's process of renovating of your mind takes, just remember, with God the end of something is always better than the beginning. Anything that God changes ends up looking, feeling, and operating better than it did before the change.

chapter seven
dismantling learned behavior

First glances as a newborn began our mental journey, an odyssey based on visual perception of our surroundings. From that point until now, we have received and processed immeasurable amounts of information. Information plays a large part in the development of our beliefs and opinions. As humans, we often do what we do and say what we say because of what we have learned through observation or experience. Our encounters with good and bad inform our perceptions and fuel our reactions to life's moments.

The concept of good versus bad isn't given much consideration by a child until he understands the corresponding consequences. Typically, he won't express remorse until there is a clearly defined explanation of wrongdoing. The internal process of differentiating between good and bad decisions and their corresponding consequences is typically not solidified in the early stages of life. Whether we understood fully or not, we have been learning ever since we were born. During that time we develop opinions, behaviors, perspectives, and eventually build our beliefs on experiential knowledge.

I Didn't Realize I Learned That

Ever wondered how habits develop? Habit formation can be defined as the process of learning a specific behavior. Forming a habit requires practice or rehearsal of a response to some form of stimuli. Opinions vary on how much repetition, whether mental or motor, constitutes habit formation. The learning process begins when you repeatedly encounter stimuli that produce positive or negative reactions. Positive reactions yield an overwhelmingly positive outlook and the ability to cope or recover. Negative reactions in time can become routine and eat away at a person's emotional, physiological, and spiritual health. If left unchecked, the negative downturn repeatedly occurs until there is little or no inhibition or internal warning. In spiritual terms, a person eventually develops numbness to the ingredients of sin and unrighteousness. Sin becomes a habit. Habits lead to addictions and addictions are hard to break. Breaking an addiction takes therapy, and in many cases a process of detoxification. Renovating the mind is God's way of therapy and enables us to accurately access what needs to be fixed about the way we think so that we become more like God.

Learning Through Repetition

How many songs have you learned because you heard the lyrics repeatedly? When I like a song I tend to play it over and over again. It eventually becomes a part of my daily experience. I might even find myself humming it while mowing the grass or washing the car. As learners we retain what we come to love.

For example, music lovers can become more familiar with a song while performing other tasks like driving or exercising. Passive aural retention has occurred when lyrics are imprinted in the listener's memory, often without their active participation. What we choose to listen to and retain can affect us. For instance, if a person was reared in a verbally abusive atmosphere, at one time their outlook on life might have been void of hope and full of frustration. Ultimately, it is their decision to change for the better or worse. It's up to them to break the cycle of mental torment and sub-par living. It boils down to whether they have had enough and are willing to take the chance to change. Because of Jesus' sacrifice, past issues and battles lack the power to stifle God's progress in anyone who believes in Him.

It Might Benefit Me Anyway...

Passive aural attention also has its benefits. To better prepare myself to communicate in today's culture, I take Spanish lessons while driving. There are numerous learning-based podcasts and lectures on Apple's iTunes that offer free educational content for personal enrichment. I consciously choose to learn Spanish passively because I don't have the time right now to take a course. Others describe this type of learning as multi-task learning. Even if you decide to passively learn some new things, keep your mind open to hearing from God. Beware of becoming so busy that communing daily with God gets demoted on your priority list. Make sure that you are mentally available for God to speak. True listeners always hear what others wish they had heard.

See and Hear

Eyes are an important key to developing behavior, whether good or bad. While many learn aurally, others learn by watching. Most learn by a combination of both. According to Luke 11:34 theeyes are the light of the body. If you focus on God, your body will be filled with His light, which conditions you to be a worthy vessel for His work. On the other hand, if you enjoy looking for and at what God's abhors, you condition yourself to agree with the devil and dwell in darkness. Satan attempts his most destructive work in dark-filled people, places and things. Remember that your body is the temple of the Holy Spirit. Where there is light, darkness cannot reside.

Luke 11:34 also discloses that a Spirit-owned mind is filled with the knowledge of God. This knowledge is gathered by way of the eye. Your whole body will be filled with light when you remember that God's light always leads to doing what is right.

Let Your Little Light Shine

Total surrender to Jesus Christ nets us a light-filled soul. The more we experience Jesus Christ as Lord and Savior, the more light can flood the soul. Knowledge of God is the light that catches the attention of others seeking truth and righteousness. Their eyes become drawn to the light they detect in you. Do everything you can to glow for God.

This little light of mine
I'm gonna let it shine
This little light of mine
I'm gonna let it shine
Let it shine, let it shine
Let it shine!

I often wondered why people sneak glances at me and my wife Marcia. We seem to garner a lot of attention. It's not because we are uber-fabulous. We aren't famous. We don't wear the trendiest clothes. On morning, while in prayer, God gave me the reason for the attention. God revealed that His presence in our lives was causing others to take interest. Marcia and I understand that we don't look good in and of ourselves. God in His graciousness cloaks us in righteousness as a result our sincere relationship with him. It's the Jesus in us that draws

70

the attention. We try our best to be holy as He is holy. We subscribe to God's way of life for us.

Free Subscription

To subscribe to something means to agree with it. Agreeing with God is perhaps the best choice a person could ever make. Endorsing what God is doing causes Him to in turn endorse what you are attempting to accomplish. If righteousness is your goal, then faith in God gets you there. Subscribing to God's way disarms satan and renders him totally ineffective. Darkness and evil have no chance if you subscribe to God's will for your life. Included in your subscription is the infusion of all your thinking with the Light of God. In Philippians 4: 8, the apostle Paul elaborates on light-filled thinking.

> And now, dear brothers and sisters, one final thing. Fix your thoughts on what is true, and honorable, and right, and pure, and lovely, and admirable. Think about things that are excellent and worthy of praise.

The Truth About Truth

Satan truly believes he has an answer for or better version of everything God designs and sets forth. He wants you to believe him more than God. Paul's advice doesn't tell us to focus on things that pertain to darkness-satan's realm of operation. Consider that he is the father of darkness and all who sin willfully and stubbornly are his children. Everything satan is and will ever be is a lie. To keep him bound and impotent, focus your thoughts and energy what is true. Why? Because it is impossible for satan to tell the truth since he is the very opposite of what God stands for.

In John 8:32 says that, "ye shall know the truth, and the

truth shall make you free." The Greek word for *truth* in this verse is *aletheia* which means things appertaining or relating to God. Truth is defined as respect for God and placing the execution of His will and purposes as an utmost priority. Truth is freedom from falsehood and deceit.

Sally wants to be free from lying and deceitfulness. She works tirelessly trying to rid herself of these sins. However, she does not pray consistently nor does she attend church regularly. Neither does she tithe. Her relationship with God is at best a cycle of inconsistency. Obviously, Sally is not operating in whatsoever is true, which denotes things pertaining directly to God. Unfortunately, she will continue to experience difficulty if a reverential fear and respect for God and His will for her life is not developed.

Must Sally know every detail of His plan for her life immediately? No, but she would do herself a great service by honoring God with prayer and her financial substance consistently. I'm sure God will then offer revelation and spiritual strategy. Operating in truth will cause Sally to be filled with light and positioned to receive God's manifold blessings for her life.

In God there is an abundance of many things, including truth. As Moses prepared to receive the Commandments of God a second time, he was instructed to take two tablets of stone with him to Mount Sinai. While on Sinai, the Lord passes before Moses and describes himself. God is "merciful, gracious, longsuffering, and abundant in goodness and truth" (Exodus 34:6). Because of who He is, God desires to pour much more truth into you. God never runs out of truth. Diligently seek after truth for the rest of your life.

The truth you discover in God always points to even greater truth. The question is whether you earnestly desire to be a carrier and dispenser of His truth and to be a God-inspired thinker.

The Chief Benefit Of Truth

In my estimation the crux of truth is freedom. Mental, physical, and social freedom is attained by adhering to God's truth. John 8:32 is the quintessential passage outlining this chief benefit, "And ye shall know the truth, and the truth shall make you free." It is interesting that more people don't take advantage of this great offer. I wonder if some people really understand that embracing truth has awesome benefits. Freedom is precious. Freedom is desirable. Freedom is worth fighting for. Freedom is not free. Ask modern day persecuted Christian missionaries, especially in non-Christian countries, about the importance of freedom. Their testimonies are bound to shift your perspective.

Simply put, your mental renovation will cost you. But look at the bright side, everything you don't need has been bought for a hefty price. Sin caused by dark thinking is totally expendable. However, as sinners we purchased many of our difficulties with disobedience. Nevertheless, the Blood of Jesus purchased our salvation and the ability to live free of terrible weights and stinking thinking. A better life is yours for the taking. Renovating your mind involves subscribing to the truth of God's Word and not doubting His ability or willingness to do what it says He will do. So, is your ultimate freedom worth changing the way you perceive and receive? Moses thought so.

The Israelites were in slavery over four-hundred years to an harsh Egyptian system and its Pharoh. The Bible reports the Egyptians made the Hebrews serve with rigor. (Exodus 1:13). Pharaoh's decree to kill all male Israelite children and exponentially increase their workload was a direct result of his ignorance and insecurity as a leader. He was fearful that those he had enslaved would grow in number, side with his enemies, and overthrow his empire. However, the more the Jews were afflicted the more they grew in number and strength.

While in Egypt the Israelites were a mighty nation who had not yet tapped into the truth of who they really were. They needed to be reminded of their identity. God had set aside a place for His people. It was a land flowing with milk and honey that contained every provision they needed to sustain successful lives. They were actually a people designed to conquer any pending obstacles. They were created to be free. Abraham was an example of the prosperity that the Israelites were supposed to experience. Nevertheless, in Genesis we find them broken and in captivity until God eventually sends Moses back to Egypt to liberate His people, the Israelites.

God's promise to truth bearers is that He will exalt them to positions of honor. He will even cause their enemies be at peace with them. We can see this promise come to pass in the life of Moses. God charged him with the monumental task of being His representative to Israel. God exalted Moses to the position of national leader to institute a mentality of freedom and prosperity among the Israelites. As the Israelites moved closer and closer to the Promised Land, their awareness of the truth of God also grew. Yes, they did rebel against God by serving other gods. But God continued to show His love and preference for Israel as His chosen people.

Moses met with God face to face in Exodus 33:11 and was therefore qualified to walk in authority; to be used as an instrument of God assigned to others' lives. Truth is often hard to accept because walking in God's truth causes you to face the facts.

Assessing Self

Personal assessment is of great benefit to those who desire true change. Plato said, "The unexamined life is not worth living." Renovating your mind involves self-examination, assessment, and discovery. Assessing your problem doesn't have to be as painful as you might think. The Holy Spirit is more than willing to help during your quest for mental freedom. To productively assess yourself you must be willing to confess and repent for bad, ungodly thoughts. Also of great importance is the opening of your mind to be filled with what God desires and staying out of condemnation.

Confessing Bad Thoughts

1 John 1:9 announces that if you confess your sins, then Jesus is ready to forgive you and cleanse you from all unrighteousness. What a guarantee. If you open your mouth and tell God the truth about yourself, He will restore you. Not only can you tell God, which by the way is the best way, you can confess your sins to a trusted family member or friend. James 5: 16 says, "Confess your faults one to another, and pray one for another, that ye may be healed. The effectual fervent prayer of a righteous man avails much." Confessing your faulty thinking to those you trust garners prayer in your favor. Someone else earnestly praying for your condition is a great way for things to positively change. God always answers sincere, unselfish prayers.

Repenting For Bad Thoughts

Charles Swindoll defines repentance as "a change of reaction from defense to a full acknowledgment. From an attempt to excuse one's sin to an absolute and unguarded realization and admission that the whole of it was wrong, accompanied with a desire never to repeat it." For your repentance to hold water a desire to abstain from improper thoughts, and what stimulates them, must be developed. If that means refraining from certain people, places, or things, then so be it. It is better to pay now, through obedience to God, rather than ante up with interest later. Look at what David asked God to do after improper thoughts led him into sin.

> Wash me clean from my guilt. Purify me from my sin. For I recognize my shameful deeds – they haunt me day and night. Against you, and you alone,　　have I sinned; I have done what is evil in your sight. You will be proved right in what you say, and your judgment against me is just. For I was born a sinner – yes, from the moment my mother conceived me. But you desire honesty from the heart, so you can teach me to be wise in my inmost being (Psalm 51: 2-6 NLT)

Open Your Mind

Imagine you're driving along and suddenly notice that your gas tank is almost empty. You say to yourself, "I don't have time to stop now. I know I have enough gas to make it home. I've been here before." How many people do you know whose tanks are always nearly empty? Perhaps, there are three types of believers:

Full Believers - they obey God's word and submit to His will all the time.

Half-Full Believers - they only disobey on occasion or only when convenient.

Empty Believer -they always operate on fumes—causing perpetual frustration, depression, and denial.

Actually, being empty is not so bad after all. God is strong especially when we're our weakest. The emptier you are the more God by his Spirit can pour into you. But, let's not forget the importance of being full. God will keep pouring until you overflow. He desires that you overflow with his love, mercy, grace, kindness, peace, joy, and happiness. Greatness is birthed in the Kingdom when His attributes in you spill over onto someone else's life. Opening your mind means being available to his Spirit so that you resist the condemnation of satan and are positioned to show others His way.

Don't Fall For It: Condemnation

Romans 8:1 says, "therefore, there is now no condemnation for those who are in Christ Jesus." This verse is actually a continuation of Romans Chapter 7. The Apostle Paul gives thanks that he is a slave (servant) of God's law and exposes his utter reliance on Christ. We are justified by faith in Christ, which makes satan's condemnation and accusations of no effect. When condemnation is not a factor the plans and purposes of God come into focus and serve as a catalyst for the next level of living in freedom.

The process of mental renovation is worth it because God has a plan for you. His plan has you blessed to be a blessing. You must obtain your freedom to assist others with getting theirs. God's truth is freedom. Walk abundantly and securely in it.

Think On the Ultimate Example

Honestly, it is sometimes difficult to conceive of a mind filled with the awesome things listed in this book as benefits of a renovated mind. Truthfully, it would be nearly impossible to envision them without an image in the form of an example. To accomplish what Paul suggests in Philippians 4:8 takes intentional effort. Because we are constantly bombarded with images, situations, and relationships that in many ways frame what we think, who we are, and how we react, we must be vigilant in the pursuit of a renovated mind.

Honesty 101

Operating honestly can be difficult only because of man's sinful nature. There is certainly a fine line between being brutally honest and executing honesty with the love of Christ. Similarly to truth, honesty begins with you. Figuratively speaking, your mental house must be swept and in order if others are to benefit from your transformation.

The word *honest* is derived from the Latin word *honestus* which implies honor. An honest thing is reputable, praiseworthy, free from fraud, respectable, and creditable. So the mandate to think on honest things entails adapting our thought processes to things that produce images and thoughts that are reputable and respectable.

I confess that in our fallen society there is much distraction, deceit, and destruction. However, God has still surrounded mankind with His awesomeness. God is the Creator of all that is good. The problem is that it seems as if the bad is more interesting. Take a moment to call to mind a few things that are praiseworthy. Ponder these questions:

- Is my relationship with God creditable?
- Do I possess any praiseworthy, Godly attributes?
- What can I do to fill my thinking with fraud-less thoughts?
- Can others see God at work in me?
- Am I helping or hurting God's reputation?
- Does how I think beautify and set me apart to holiness?

A Matter Of Integrity

Another aspect of honest thinking has to do with integrity. Have you ever thought about buying an item that was not registered? I have. Years ago God dealt with me about purchasing "hot" items from "street brokers." These desirable items had no serial numbers and many could not be traced. You might know at least one person who can "hook you up." When I was interested in getting things at an extremely discounted price I thought about doing it constantly. I was always looking for the next opportunity. In reality I was not thinking on things of integrity. Why? Those things I cherished so much were stolen goods. Because I enjoyed getting a great deal I would methodically talk myself into purchasing items, even though I knew it was wrong.

A goal for any person should be to live what they teach. Part and parcel with that is becoming a person who does what they say. It is important not to delve into hypocrisy. Honesty with others while helping them reach their potential pleases God.

Living a live of integrity governed by godly thoughts has much to do with self-reflection. Many Christians fall prey to integrity-less thinking. For instance, duplicating music or videos for personal or business distribution is against the law. Yet, a movie can be released in theatres on Friday. Saturday morning it's for sell on DVD. Those who perpetuate the black market can't possibly harbor honest thoughts. Integrity in thought leads to integrity in action. Pondering honest things means thinking thoughts and planning actions that build up rather than destroy, that nurture rather that abuse, and that ultimately give God glory. It is thinking on whatever is worthy of reverence.

Reverencing the Redeemer

At the top of every believer's list of things or people to reverence should be Jesus Christ. Take a few moments to mediate on exactly what Jesus has done for you. If you have any doubts or don't know read any of the Gospels: Matthew, Mark, Luke, or John. Afterward you should easily answer the following:

- Besides Jesus, has anyone ever died for you and your sins?
- Besides Jesus, has anyone ever died and handed you ev erything you needed to be successful?

Probably not. God loved you so much that He made the ultimate sacrifice so that, if you believe on who was sacrificed, you won't take your last breath without having life beyond this life (John 3:16; paraphrased by author).

Reverencing Christ means submitting your thinking to Him. Let His thoughts about you and your circumstances consume you. He is more than up for the task.

Images

An image is a tangible or visible representation of something. It can also be a mental picture of something not actually present or something that produces an attitude based on interaction. I would combine all these meanings to define an image as a tangible representation of something good or bad that produces a mental picture that informs the observer through perception, consequently forming a belief or attitude.

Simply put, images are points of learning that inform behavior. In Scripture, God wastes no time revealing His attitude toward images that caused men to behave poorly. In Exodus 20: 4, God says:

> "You shall not make for yourself a carved image, or any likeness of anything that is in heaven above, or that is in the earth beneath, or that is in the water under the earth."

In Deuteronomy 4:23, God says:

Take heed to yourselves, lest you forget the covenant of the Lord your God which He made with you, and make for yourselves a carved image in the form of anything which the Lord your God has forbidden you.

In essence, God wants to be our image. After all you were made in His image and likeness (Genesis 1:26). We are exposed to a tremendous variety of information. For the vast majority of life our brains are at work processing signals and promptings from internal and external sources. Whether we recognize it or not we are constantly exposed to tainted or corrupted images. Images of grandeur and success without God are just the tip of the iceberg. Any image that does not give God glory nor positively enrich your experience with Him is not worth your time.

The Images You Adopt Determine Your Image

Another definition of image has to do with people's perception of you. I hear people frequently say, "I won't do or say that. It will ruin my image." Unfortunately, for many, public perception is everything. For them life is based upon facades, fixes, compromising relationships, and deceit. Instead of allowing Jesus to be their ultimate image, they settle for flesh-comfort and self-denial. They are intimidated by the unknown. What is the unknown? It is a life sacrificed to the will of God. In reality, new life is only unknown until you allow God to make Himself known to you.

It is sad thing to watch people construct their lives around images garnered from music, videos, celebrities, commercials, and such. Generally, people tend to act like what they see and experience constantly. This is not to suggest that all images are negative, just the ones that do not give God glory. A recent covert plan of the enemy has been the bombardment of the public with images that conjure up thoughts of failure. The enemy only wants you to be successful to a certain point. After that, if success was built according to his plan, disaster is imminent. God's plan for you is not centered on what has made you wrong. It is based on who has made you right. Everything concerning you in God is centered on Jesus and His work on behalf of all men. The devil desires to pervert or totally destroy the effects of the ultimate sacrifice made by Jesus for you. One way the enemy attempts to accomplish his plan is with thoughts of failure and negativity.

Constant negativity usually results in a tendency to be negative. Unless one intentionally decides otherwise, the onslaught of emotion can come to govern and thwart the joy-filled life God intends for all. How you perceive yourself and your surroundings has a great deal to do with your relationship with God, family, friends, and co-workers. In fact your relationship with God or lack thereof is packed full of choices. Deuteronomy 11: 26-28 says:

> "Behold, I set before you today a blessing and a curse: the blessing, if you obey the commandments of the Lord your God which I command you today; and the curse, if you do not obey the commandments of the Lord your God, but turn aside from the way which I command you today, to go after other gods which you have not known."

Almost as heart wrenching as observing people build thinking and lifestyles based on tainted imagery is watching people suffer from learned behavior sparked by terrible habits exhibited by parents, relatives, and friends. These learned behaviors are often referred to as generational curses.

Personally, I am on a mission to make sure that my children never repeat the mistakes I made. I constantly come before the Lord with Psalm 51 on my lips. I do not desire past sin, which have been accounted for by the blood of Jesus, to manifest itself in my present. I personally believe that from the point of conception a child begins to learn from its environment. Let me prove my theory. Let's say you have a pregnant woman who has a terrible habit of smoking and excessive drinking. Studies have proven that those behaviors can severely increase the probability of numerous problems for the unborn child.

Bad choices are fueled by improper thinking and bad perception. As an adolescent I had a terrible perception of the world around me. I had no idea until much in life that I was gripped with a fear of failure. That spirit of failure was so embedded in my character I tried everything I could to assimilate. My assimilation into what I thought was cool and beneficial to me was attained through the compromising of my relationship with Christ. Even as a youngster, I knew the voice of God but didn't listen. As you can imagine I ended up lost in sin and spiritual degradation. I was so interested in fitting in and being the topic of discussion I relinquished, through my thinking, my rightful place as a blessed and favored instrument of God. So, I began my journey through sexual sin, hypocrisy, deceit, and rebellion. If only I had made Jesus my choice. But I didn't trust Him like I desired to be trusted by people who actually didn't have my best interest at heart. I eventually became like what I surrounded myself with. I ended up deriving my identity from tainted sources and eventually formed a false sense of integrity. I became an expert at building facades. On the outside everything looked good, but I was literally dying on the inside.

Enough Is Enough

It took time for me to resolve within myself that a lifestyle of sin was no longer an option. Once I realized who warped my think was, I pledged to never return to it ever again. It took God to get me out and it takes God to keep me out. If you are suffering where you are, resolve right now to allow God to change you. Be steadfast in your commitment to grow in God. He is the lover of you soul and there is nothing He desires more than to empower you to live authentically for Him. We are His models. We have been chosen to walk through life shinning and advertising for His love, grace, power, and joy. Loving God with all you heart makes you attractive to those who need Him.

It is our responsibility to ensure that those we have been entrusted to be stewards over are given every benefit in Christ. When is the last time someone came to Christ as a result of watching how you operate as a Christian? Is your life representative of life in Christ? We have many decisions to make along our journey toward spiritual maturity. We have the choice of life or death, blessings or curses. No one can shove you to Jesus. Those who have been shoved, usually rebel and end up worse off than before they came. But you have the awesome opportunity to dismantle learned behavior. Renovating the mind presents the chance to set the record straight, square your shoulders, and stand firm in liberty through Jesus Christ.

chapter eight
making Godly decisions

Any successful renovation includes the making of several important decisions. These choices determine whether the renovation will produce pleasing results. A typical construction projects requires that decisions be made relating to budget, materials, and personnel. After assessing what needs to be accomplished, a plan of action in the form of a blueprint is produced. The blueprint allows for strategic planning and time management. Renovations that run off schedule always run over budget. It seems as if people these days rarely contemplate life as one-time event. We only get one chance at this, so why not do it right? People plan to fail because they fail to plan. In fact, believers plan in partnership with God's Spirit to ensure the best possible outcome.

Meeting With the General Contractor

To receive the highest quality product, your newly renovated mind, regular meetings with the General Contractor are required. In the natural this might happen three times a week at most. In the spiritual realm the meeting should happen several times a day. How do we communicate with the GC (God)? We maintain effective communication and communion with

God through prayer, meditation, and worship.

Jesus said in John 10:27 that "My sheep listen to my voice, I know them, and they follow me." Without constant communication with God, the decision making process during your mental renovation can be hindered by discouragement, deceit, and distraction.

Indeed, you lead a busy life. Maybe you think there are legitimate reasons not to spend time with God. Actually, those reasons are really just excuses. To communicate well with God, develop a hunger for His presence. That yearning hunger is nurtured in a heart that desires to pray.

Have A Little Talk

Prayer is the primary means of communication with God. Prayer has great benefits for the believer. It provides strength to resist temptation and to grow into the image of Christ. Further, prayer changes the world while giving you the opportunity to confess sins and receive forgiveness. Prayer also cultivates a loving submission to the will of God and even promotes the message of Jesus Christ. It empowers you to make better decisions. Making sound decisions now to assures that a quality renovation of your mind occurs. If the General Contractor has to go back and make corrections after the process is completed, it will cost you. Prayers are only answered after you pray them. After seeking God, you will undoubtedly grow in love and your willingness to submit to His will.

Allow God to continue His work in you by His Spirit. Communication with God is a two-way street. As you develop a thriving inner-life through prayer, study, and Spirit-led meditation the power of God will bless your life.

Think On These Things

Meditation is an ancient spiritual discipline. It is a means of communicating with God through silence, simplicity, and stillness. Over the years meditation has received bad press from Christians, mostly as a result of misconception. There indeed are many forms of meditation that span several religions. However, I want to offer a brief explanation of how Christian meditative practices benefit the renovation of the mind. The goal of meditation is to leave your mind and the thoughts it contains in a different, more God-ward state than when you started. It's important that you meet and greet God every morning before anyone else. For example, when I get up in the morning, my initial movement is not toward the edge of the bed. My first action is to be still. Immediately I thank God for allowing me to experience another day. I want the first of every new day to be with God. After being with Him first, I am always ready to handle whatever I encounter for the rest of the day.

A result of that quiet time with God is meditation. I usually meditate on a passage or verse of Scripture I read the night before. Sometimes I lie awake, communing with God, for almost an hour before starting any aspects of the day. I remain faithful to this routine because I am fully aware that as soon as my feet hit the floor the busy day commences. Dietrich Bonhoeffer had this to say about meditation:

> When we awake, we drive away the dark shapes and confused dreams of the night as we speak the morning blessing and commend ourselves for this day to the triune God. The evil moods, uncontrollable emotions and desires, which we cannot get rid of during the day, are often enough simply ghosts of the night that were not driven off in the morning and now want to spoil the day for us. The first moments of the new day are not for our own plans and worries, not even for our zeal to accomplish our own work, but for God's liberating grace, God's sanctifying presence...Before the heart unlocks itself for the world, God wants to open it for

himself…

Meditating on Scripture allows you to take the Word of God with you throughout the day. The Word of God becomes a portable weapon to defeat every scheme of the enemy. You are more apt to apply something you're already thinking about. As your mind becomes more and more renewed through renovation, you come to realize the extreme importance of daily conversation with God. In that exchange between you and God, He desires your total, undivided attention.

Concentrate Please

A key component of effective Holy Spirit-led meditation is concentration. An un-renovated mind is a mind that mindlessly wanders. Those who have not yet been transformed by renewing their mind and thoughts have a difficult time with committing to anything substantive for a sustained period of time. Experts suggest that for the benefits of mediation to become evident, one must serious engage the mind for a minimum of thirty minutes. This premise can be applied to other activities people regularly engage in. Any respectable personal trainer will tell you in order to loose weight you must eat properly and maintain an exercise regimen. A portion of that fitness program must include sustained cardiovascular activity, usually performed at least three days a week. To stay the course focus and discipline are needed. Discipline opens the door for concentration. Becoming comfortable with mediation will only happen if you train yourself to view it as an indispensable part of your lifestyle.

A Misconception

Mediation is not synonymous with Bible study. However,

it is a product of serious biblical study. The examination and internalization of scripture is indeed a vital aspect of mental renovation. Don't stop at surface reading and studying of God's Word. Endeavor to go deeper in your understanding and application the Word. Study to show yourself approved to Him. After searching and allowing God's truth to permeate your life then allow God-guided meditation to embed the precepts and meanings of Scripture in your thinking. Meditation is the means for internalizing what you encounter in Scripture.

Worth the Wait

There is an aspect of meditation that gives rise to its unpopularity among some Christians. We live in a fast paced society that teaches us that waiting for anything is akin to wasting time. Microwaves specialize in preparing in minutes what used to take hours. Contrary to present cultural norms, there is an inherent element of waiting in meditation. No matter what the surroundings suggest, it's okay to wait on God. He may not speak when we want Him to, but when He decides to, in His infinite wisdom, His words shouldn't be taken lightly. When He speaks, be ready to listen. Allow the life-defining words God offers to ramp up your desire to further commune with Him, especially in worship.

Worshipping Him Truthfully

We cannot imagine that the church gathers for worship on Sunday morning if by this we mean that we then engage in something that we have not been engaging in the rest of the week. - D.A. Carson

Worshipping God is vital to the mental renovation process. It is impossible to renew the mind without worshipping the One who created it. As God's creation we inherently possess a need to express how we feel about Him. That need is a part of who we are.

There are various corporate expressions of worship ranging from traditional to contemporary to emergent and so on. Churches worldwide typically embrace the type of worship expression that ministers to their spiritual sphere of influence. Despite religious affiliation, the reality is that everyone should worship God. God desires that all His creation adore and reverence Him. In John 4:23-24 we learn that God is looking for people who will worship Him.

> But the time is coming-indeed it's here now-when true worshipper will worship the Father in spirit and in truth. The Father is looking for those who will worship him that way. For God is Spirit, so those who worship him must worship in spirit and truth.

Worship positions us to receive the divine revelation and wisdom needed for every situation we face. I like to think of worship as conversation with God. No matter your disposition, in worship He always makes the first move. Have you ever not felt like worshipping God, but knew you needed to? Have you ever skipped worship service to get those "extra" hours of sleep? Afterward, did you experience a nagging feeling of unfulfillment? If so, that was God by His Holy Spirit convicting you of your unwise decision to not worship Him when you had the chance.

There's something about communing with God that stretches far beyond what words can convey. Often the most difficult thing for a worshipper to do is to express in words what they experience during worship. True worship leaves us in awe of God. Maintaining that reverential awe is the gateway to a deeper, more profound relationship with God. For a person who loves being with God, an encounter with Him can leave them speechless. When beauty and majesty overwhelm us, words fail to do justice in providing a description of the experience.

Just for clarification. I define worship as the summation of various sacred acts directed toward God for His glorification. Many limit the concept of worship to the "praise and worship" period during a typically contemporary worship service. The praise and worship period of a given church service is but one aspect of a more expansive, all-encompassing worship experience with God.

True worship necessitates a response from the worshipper at all times. Whether it is a call to worship, responsive scriptural reading, litany, verbalization of a creed, the singing of hymns, anthems, and choruses, the worshipper must participate in the experience. God is very interested, during worship, in our response to His greatness, not the greatness of men.

Metaphorically, worshipping God happens in mystery and through story. And that worship is an ongoing event. It should occur consistently, inside and outside of a weekly church gathering. In essence, worship is a lifestyle, not an event.

Relationship Introduces Mystery

The term *mystery* denotes a religious belief based on divine revelation, especially one regarded as beyond human understanding. The language of mystery is wrapped in our relationship with God as all-mighty and all-powerful. Any communication with Him should at least address those attributes. Mystery keeps us from vainly ascending mentally to God. Many learned and educated people have struggled to maintain their sanity while trying to figure out God. They fail to realize that it is impossible to know everything about God. He doesn't think or act like us. There is much about God that is mystery and can only be discovered through intimate relationship with Him. Therefore, the correct response to the mysteriousness of God is awe. No man can be prepared for the full revelation of God while still residing in temporality. Moses never saw God face to face, just the back of Him as He passed by. We can't handle the pure essence of God in an imperfect state. No man has ever seen God, but we all can experience Him. The more we worship Him the more we will come to know about Him.

We will have the blessed opportunity to experience the fullness of God upon entering into eternal life. However, now in our present reality we can understand God more through worship. As you allow God to permeate your consciousness and will, your mind and thoughts move higher and further from the reach of satan. Worshipping God is salient to mental renovation. Develop a constant desire to be transformed and transitioned in the presence of God.

And so, dear brothers and sisters, I plead with you to give your bodies to God because of all he done for you. Let them be a living and holy sacrifice-the kind he will find acceptable. This is truly the way to worship him. Don't copy the behavior and customs of this world, but let God transform you into a new person by changing the way you think. Then you will learn to know God's will for you, which is good and pleasing and perfect (Romans 12:1-2).

Worship Through Story

Satan wins if he can convince you to worship Jesus Christ as something other than He is. Many religious communities and movements do not place the emphasis on Jesus Christ as Christians do. Islam along with other religions, recognize Jesus, but not as Lord and Savior. In the midst of your renovation, worshipping Christ as the perfect, infallible expression of love from God takes on a mode of thanksgiving. Jesus, through His suffering and death, paid the price for each of us. The text of the hymn *Jesus Paid It All* sums up well Jesus' atoning work:

> *Jesus paid it all*
> *All to Him I owe*
> *Sin has left a crimson stain*
> *He washed me white as snow*

Worshipping through story lead us an irrevocable appreciation of the story of Jesus and His impact on our lives. Personally, I read and study the story of Jesus' crucifixion at least three times a year. I need a full-blown reminder of the ridicule, shame, assault, and blame Jesus Christ took for me. Jesus' blood that was shed for all humanity still has power today. Being reminded of the sacrifice God made for my life keeps me grounded and thankful. What Jesus did, paired with what the Holy Spirit is doing, empowers you to lay down unproductive, ill-fated thoughts. Honestly, all have sinned and come short of God's glory (Romans 3:23). You're not perfect, yet you have the opportunity and right to change your mind and shift it from what has prevented you from being who God created you to be.

Step Up

Now is the time to step into your promised place. Because your mind is being renewed, coming are opportunities to experience God in new and exciting ways. You have a divine purpose. In fact, you have always possessed a divine purpose, it just had to be revealed as you progressed through God's renovation process.

To ensure success you must commit to an ever-growing relationship with the General Contractor. Remember, the GC is God. He has supervised the process from day one. You must succeed. Why? Because God wants to make an example of you. He has something to prove to all those who don't believe in his Word and His Son Jesus Christ-that all things are possible if you believe.

chapter nine
a new boldness

With immorality increasingly rampant in churches and Christian organizations, it seems as if we have abdicated ourselves from standing for truth and integrity. The most powerful institution in the world is God's Church. We are called out—the *ekklesia*. Today's Church is being called out of its comfort zone into the world to make a difference, not to sit passively as the surrounding culture defines our existence. Walking unashamed and with boldness places us in position to shine our light into darkness. In 1 Peter 1:6-7 we find,

> So be truly glad. There is wonderful joy ahead, even though you have to endure many trials for a little while. These trials will show that your faith is genuine. It is being tested as fire tests and purifies gold—though your faith is far more precious than mere gold. So when you faith remains strong through many trials, it will bring you much praise and glory and honor on the day when Jesus Christ is revealed to the whole world.

2 Timothy 1:7-8 also speaks to maintaining a positive perspective.

> For God has not given us a spirit of fear and timidity, but

of power, love, and self-discipline. So never be ashamed to tell others about our Lord. And don't be ashamed of me, either, even though I'm in prison for him. With the strength God gives you, be ready to suffer with me for the sake of the Good News.

From these passages we are reminded that God has never desired for us to give up while doing His will, especially when it benefits someone else. The renovated mind is by no means consumed by adverse threats, circumstances, or situations. It is acceptable to be aware of those threats, circumstances, or situations, but not to the point where they hinder your walk with God. You are embarking on this mental renovation because God has allowed it. God desires for you to operate in the authority given through His Son Jesus Christ. Operating in God's authority, by the power of the name of Jesus Christ, empowers you to become a change-agent personally and socially. True change agents don't shy away from a good challenge.

Being bold takes courage. It's involves operating with tenasity and an assurance that we are backed by someone more powerful than we are. This boldness doesn't surface overnight. It is the result of concentrated effort combined with submission to God's will. We become bold and powerful vessels of God through submission to Him.

Power To Get It Done

Boldness is a by-product of the power of God. God's power and authority is a part of who He is. Everything God accomplishes He does so by and through His power. Everything you have accomplished in Him has been because His grace, mercy, and power co-mingled with your willingness to get something done for Him. There is no limit to what God can do with a willing heart and receptive mind. He has given us everything we need to live boldly before others. 2 Peter 1:3 says,

> According as his divine power hath given unto us all things
> that pertain unto life and godliness, through the knowledge
> of him that hath called us to glory and virtue.

Through His power God has given to us all we need to lead a productive, God-fearing life. God has given us the power to change. As we change, others around us begin to change. Situations around us begin to change. Change always begins with a thought. That thought must be powerful enough to institute a desire for something greater and more worthwhile.

The enemy's desire is for you to never have thoughts about positive change. If he can control your thoughts he can control your desires. He wants you to ponder, consider, imagine, and believe ungodly things. If satan is allowed access to your thought life he has the ability to skew your perspective. Once our perspective is tainted then we begin to see things God never intended for us to see. We commence responding to unholy stimuli that eventually create a cycle of mental degredation and ultimately mental distruction. An un-renovated mind is the playground of the devil.

To combat these mental inclinations, God has given us everything that pertains to godliness and good character. But, you can't hide behind masks and facades because the thought of people witnessing your mental transformation embarrasess you.

You Can't Hide

An un-renovated mind avoids consistent thinking about godly things. When I was "in the world" I knew of God. I confessed Jesus as Lord and was baptized. However, for years I decided to play the ignorant card. Deep down I knew what was right and pleasing to God, but ignored every inclination to adhere. As a matter of fact, I knew from my teenage years that I was called to preach the Gospel. Nevertheless, I made decisions that subjugated God's will to my personal will. Actually, I was not as ignorant as I made myself out to be. I was playing a game with myself more so than with God.

I was having great fun while slipping further and further from God. Yes, God still loved me, although at times I didn't understand it because my mind was un-renovated. I was consumed with making poor decisions that made my carnal, human nature comfortable. Consequently, I suffered spiritually. Giving too much attention to selfish desires counteracts spiritual growth and development.

It wasn't until I made a conscious decision to rededicate my life to Christ and submit to His will that I noticed true personal improvement. In reality, when I was parading sin before the world, I was ashamed of God. A sin-parade always has spectators. Inside I was a total wreck and in an incredible amount of denial. I always knew about the sacrifice Jesus made, but it didn't hit home until I made the decision to change.

Change was not easy. I eventually found myself willing to accept God's plan for my life. His plan is perfect. Because mind and spirit constantly battle, I had to be taught through God's grace to not war against God's help, but to war against the real enemy, satan. In the process of change I realized that I had a purpose and wanted to be an example for others. I developed a hunger for intimacy with God. From that intimacy grew a desire to represent Jesus and build others. To maintain the momentum I had discovered in God, I needed to constantly be refreshed and renewed in my thought life. Always strive to be an example of Christ to others. To be that glowing example, you can't be ashamed of God and His Word.

"Let your light shine before men so that they may see your good works and glorify your Father in Heaven" (Matthew 5:16).

I recently discovered a term that describes the bold attitude that you and I must operate in if we're going to possess all God has for us. If we are going to lay hold of the bountiful blessings of God for our lives we must be unabashed. Being unabashed means that we are not embarrassed. It also means that we are confident and undaunted. Things that used to sway us away from God no longer have the power to distract us. We can no longer allow our priorities to get mixed up. An renovated mind puts first things first. God is important and should be placed at the forefront of our lives.

C.S. Lewis once said, "Christianity, if false, is of no importance, and if true, of infinite importance. The only thing it cannot be is moderately important." If our mind deemphasizes godly behavior then we loose track of who we truly are in Christ. God gave us our identity, so that means it is vitally important to Him. Anything God creates is expected to reflect His character.

Your identity in Christ is vitally important to those around you. The Kingdom of God needs you. A renovated mind opens up a world of possibilities through Jesus. Contrary to popular belief, you cannot do all things through Christ while the mind is in disrepair. It is only after old, irrelevant ways of thinking have been demolished and swept away by God's love, can we partner with His Spirit to reshape our perception and ramp up our productivity. So, don't be ashamed or scared. God doesn't make cowards. In fact, you were created in His image and likeness. He has been and will be infusing your life with His power. This power comes in the form of authority, virtue, might, love, discipline, and self-control. They are to be used to accomplish His purposes. And to that end, rest in the fact that, in God's eyes we are always victorious.

A Natural Order

In 2 Timothy 1:7 the Apostle Paul is encouraging a young leader named Timothy. Paul uses his knowledge of God and experience with Jesus to build Timothy up for the task of leading others to Jesus Christ. To ease Timothy's mind Paul says,

> For God has not given us a spirit of fear and timidity, but of power, love, and self-discipline.

This familiar verse of Scripture outlines several principles for anyone who desires to participate in bold change. Notice in the verse that Paul reassures his protege that God didn't give them a spirit of fear. Paul immediately emphasizes what God has not given. Many times to understand and appreciate what God *has given* you must recognize what He *has not given*. The original Greek term for *not* in this verse actually means *absolutely not*.

Paul establishes what does not come from God to give Timothy a clear picture of what does. God, in His infinite wisdom, through Paul creates a natural order toward a disciplined mind. First comes the spirit of power, then of love, and finally a sound and disciplined mind.

Before we experience the benefits of a renewed and renovated mind we must recieve and operate in God's power. The power Paul is talking about in this verse is God's *dunamis* power. This power has to do with inherent power, power residing in a thing by virtue of its nature, or power which a person or thing exerts and puts forth.

By our very nature as God's beloved, we possess power and authority over everything satan stands for. Our boldness doesn't stem from our own physical ability. It is a result of the nature of God down on the inside of us to live for and serve Him with godly character and integrity.

The spirit of power also manifests itself in the love that we show God and others. The power to love God, others and ourselves has its genesis in the sacrifice Jesus made on Calvary. The power to love was perfected and dispersed when Jesus Christ conquered all His enemies. People with renovated minds love hard because they understand they are loved and forgiven. So, they never allow unforgiveness to short circuit their ability to love like Jesus did. God's agape love always leads to a mind focused on the richness of God's Word, which in turn produces a disciplined mind.

A renovated mind is a mind in order. Mental chaos itsn't allowed. When you have a renovated mind you understand that because God has unlimited power you have unlimited potential. God has given each of us potential so that it may manifest as boldness for Him.

The Necessity Of Boldness

Mental boldness eventually manifests itself as boldness of commitment and action. Being bold for God is a necessity for any believer in these days and times because of the onslaught of ungodly perceptions that define secular culture.

In reality, mental boldness is nothing more than mental toughness. This toughness is a direct result of God's desire for us to live in righteousness and power. Because we wage our fiersest battles with satan in our minds it is imperative that we operate in total assurance and dependence on the power God has given us. The mind He has given us is to be used for His glory. Operating with mental toughness allows the mind to recieve from God. It is with the mind that we receive strategy and understanding from God for abundant living.

Receiving Strategy

1 Chronicles 28 is a passage of Scripture which illustrates how God can feed the mind with His plans and strategies. Solomon, the heir apparent to the throne of Israel, is in consula-

tion with his father King David about the temple that is to be constructed in Jersusalem. David found out that he would not be allowed to reconsruct the temple because he had been a man of war who had shed the blood of many. Solomon was chosen to sit on the throne of Israel. So, he relayed specifics about how the project should be completed to his son Solomon. Verse 12 talks about how David received the information he gave to his son.

> He gave him the plans of all that the Spirit had put in his mind for the courts of the temple of the LORD and all the surrounding rooms, for the treasuries of the temple of God and for the treasuries for the dedicated things (AMP).

Everything David told Solomon came from what the Spirit of God had put into his mind. No doubt, every detail, every specification, was relayed to David's mind by God to ensure the project would be accomplished to His standard.

One of the Holy Spirit's foremost responsibilities to the believer is that of enlightenment. With God's enlightenment comes knowledge and wisdom to carryout plans with moral integrity and utmost character. David had to recognize that God was trusting him to carry valuable information and strategy. The plans that God had for the temple had to passed down to the succeeding generation to be implemented.

God desires to use our minds to pass down important information to our decendents. They have to build great things for God. Until Jesus returns we all have a part to play in furthering His agenda in the earth. In order to carry on with what we have been given we must understand what God is saying.

Because A Mind Is Open

A closed mindset is a weak mindset. For God's will to be done here on earth as it is in heaven, the mind must be open and ready to receive what He desires to communicate. God does not celebrate or bless foolishness. To be called foolish in Biblical times meant that a person was sluggish in mind and possessed dull perception.

A foolish mind leads to a warped and faithless view of what's ahead. Our perception is our point of view. It the context in which we place our thoughts, beliefs, and experiences. A foolish mind is a closed mind. A closed mind is a dark mind. A dark mind harbors thoughts that are contrary to righteousness and dependence on the power of God.

In Luke 24: 45, Jesus did something powerful. He positioned people to understand what He was saying by opening their minds.

> Then He [thoroughly] opened up their minds to understand the Scriptures, and said to them...(AMP)

Notice that before Jesus spoke words of revelation and insight He had to open their minds. Even today our minds need to be primed for God's revelation by allowing them to be receptive. In verse 46 Jesus then commences with His exposition on what He would experience and in turn what those who witnessed the coming miracle were obligated to do in response to it. Jesus was very precise and strategic.

When we meditate on what God is saying we gain better understanding and insight. An open mind to the things of God is a closed mind to the ungodly inclinations of our carnal nature. Paul warns us in Romans 8: 5 that:

> Those who live according to the flesh have their minds set on what the flesh desires; but those who live in accordance with the Spirit have their minds set on what the Spirit desires.

The flesh has it's own way of thinking. It produces thoughts that attempt reduce God's influence on our lives. The flesh is selfish and self-serving. Those who live according to it will always reap desires that tear at the fabric of true relationship and intimacy with Jesus. But, those who align their thoughts with the Spirit will always think according to what God desires. Thoughts of that type lead to God's forgiveness and favor. What the Spirit desires is the best for your life. He never desires anything that produces fear, dread, unhappiness, and disobedience.

The key to being mentally bold is a willingness to accept God's will by faith. Pair the faith with righteous works that glorify Him and that arrest everything that works against the cultivation of holiness and power. God is looking for people who are unashamed to live out loud in order to advertise His standards and expecations.

When we are bold for Him, He is even bolder for us. When we stand for righteousness and holiness, that's exactly what we shall receive. Your mental renovation is accomplished through a strong, bold desire to think differently about your destiny and how God wants to get you there.

chapter ten
higher level thinking

Present days and times require a higher level of thinking and consciousness. Old mindsets and procedures are vastly ineffective in combating the newest manifestations of sin in our culture. Consequently, society as a whole seems to be degenerating. Factors such as the economic downturn, social irresponsibility, and rampant crime, have crippled the hope of many. In times like these we need God to show up and shift the paradigm. We need a shift, a radical change, in our thinking.

The term *higher* simply denotes a more profound level of richness or extravagance. Higher-level thinking in God is not haughty or prideful. Instead, this new level of thinking is based on faith in God's ability to act supernaturally on your behalf and for the benefit of others. It is thinking rooted in the richness and power of God to solidify, by His Spirit, sustained positive change in your life. Higher-level thinking is not affected in the least by adverse circumstances. People who think at this level may be down temporarily but never out. They understand

and accept Psalm 34:19 which says, "a righteous person faces many troubles, but the Lord comes to the rescue each time."

A Timeless Mandate

There is a mandate from God which has never changed. It's that you submit yourself to God's master plan of redemption. To accomplish this victory-filled submission you must be willing to trust God now more than ever before.

Trusting God like never before leads us into places with Him we have yet to experience. He promises to lead us into greater understanding of His power so that His purposes can be accomplished. When we trust God more He trusts us with answers to prayer. He trusts you with exactly what you need and desire because He knows that your motives are rooted in what He desires. Your desires become His desires. His will becomes our will. What breaks God's heart also breaks yours too.

Through and Above

Consider two aspects of higher-level thinking. This sort of thinking produces the ability to think through and above any situation. The Holy Spirit's guidance promotes thinking through a situation without allowing it to manifest negative effects. Learning how to think through tough circumstances makes us ready to think above them. A vital aspect of thinking above the problem is the ability to believe wholeheartedly, and without reservation, that all things indeed work out for your benefit.

Thinking Through It

Difficult situations arise in all of our lives. Even the most committed, God fearing Christian experiences difficulty. Jesus put it best when He said, "I have told you all this so that you may have peace in me. Here on earth you will have many trials and sorrows. But take heart, because I have overcome the world" (John 16:33).

Jesus told His disciples that He would soon return to His Father in heaven. His discourse was intended to place their hearts and minds at peace. Jesus desired to instill in them a hope that produced a conqueror's mindset, not one of who has been conquered.

Thinking through a problem requires that you position your heart and mind so that the issue doesn't overwhelm you. Satan wants nothing more than for you to become bogged down in hopelessness and despair. Instead, approach the issue with your mind and heart saturated by God's Word. All fears and cares must be given to Jesus. If you cling to things that trouble you they eventually become access points for satan. Consistently giving Jesus your problems through prayer prompts words of faith. Confident faith about the situation sustains you even when it looks as if no change is immanent. God has promised change even when it doesn't look possible. Our responsibility in the deal is to be faithful, prayerful, and obedient in the process.

With the power of God, the Holy Spirit begins to minister solutions, even in the midst of the problem. You'll receive fresh insight and experience renewed strength despite the surrounding conditions. Thinking through a problem at a higher level gives God glory. His glory translates into a blessed assurance that you can sustain a life that pleases Him. When empowered to see what God desires you to see, you are ready to act. Pair Spirit-led actions with faith to experience God's harvest in your life.

Get Above

The second aspect of higher-level thinking is the ability and desire to think above any adverse situation. When a problem presents itself we are typically both physically and spiritually aware of it. Thinking above the problem complements thinking through the problem because as you live out the process you also understand that from a heavenly perspective that the problem is already solved. In essence, thinking above the problem is synonymous with thinking from above about the problem. Gaining and implementing a heavenly perspective keeps us from making disastrous decisions. The goal, according to the prayer Jesus taught His disciples, is to facilitate God's will being done on earth as it is in heaven, right?

Have you ever asked God what He thinks about your difficulties? When I finally mustered enough courage to ask God to give me His perspective, I was amazed at His response. What He revealed changed my life forever.

The answer to my inquiry led me to understand that I could eliminate my fears and apprehensions about what I was experiencing simply by discovering what He had already said about me in His Word. Reading about how various biblical personalities handled and triumphed over adverse circumstances catapulted my thinking above what I thought was possible. I entered into a new realm of thinking that always says, "all things are possible!"

Perspective Of Another Sort

God is everywhere all the time and He operates exclusively with a heavenly perspective. Developing a heavenly perspective takes time and work. It takes consistent prayer and a willingness to be as much like Jesus as possible. Loving, serving, and forgiving others like Jesus did can be difficult, but it's not impossible. Endeavor to become hungry for the image of Christ to reside in your life. A hunger for how heaven would handle a situation is a key ingredient in developing God-pleasing faith.

Thinking above the problem, with a perspective from heaven, means operating from a desire for the things of heaven to overcome the things of earth. In Matthew 6 when Jesus was teaching the disciples to pray He made the statement: "Your kingdom come. Your will be done on earth as it is in heaven." With that statement Jesus unleashed the importance of things on earth resembling things in heaven. If it exists in heaven, it is to be manifested on earth. Thinking above the problem allows the mind to be saturated with warfare prayers and Kingdom-building strategies that make what Jesus prayed and paid for with His blood a reality.

Still, there is another aspect of thinking above found in Ephesians 3:20.

> Now unto him that is able to do exceeding abundantly above all that we ask or think, according to the power that worketh in us...(KJV, author's emphasis)

The higher your thoughts, the more extravagant the response from God. The scripture plainly indicates that God will do exceedingly abundantly above whatever we ask or think. It sounds to me that God is ready and able to do immeasurably more than our highest thoughts about what is possible. This realm of thinking is fed by the power of God working in your life. When God's power in you meets higher-level thinking, the supernatural and miraculous occur. God specializes in being and doing more than we think is possible. Higher-level thinking, manifested by thinking above the situation, invites the best God has for your life. Elevate your thoughts to elevate your life.

Nevertheless

This higher-level of thinking is a real possibility for all born-again believers. When we received Christ as Lord and Savior we relinquished our right to harbor sin and ill-fated thoughts. Though shaped in sin, because of Adam's transgression in the garden, we have nevertheless been redeemed for a specific purpose-to bring glory to God through all that we think, say, and do. Jesus bought the clearance, with His blood, for God to communicate with us through His grace, mercy, and Word.

The term *nevertheless* is powerful for those who recognize the life they have received through Jesus Christ. While you were deeply entrenched in sin, God in His sovereign love and desire for the manifestation of your best life, sacrificed His best.

Nevertheless is a pivotal word in this process of renovation. It literally means that in spite of who you were or are now, God's love overshadows every shortcoming. The "never" in nevertheless literally means "not at all." It's a term that refutes the past while simultaneously speaking to future hope and expectation. Another way of looking at it is that because of Jesus' sacrifice you are never-the-less. So, you can look at yourself and know that you are not the least. God created you magnificently and for a divine purpose. Rest assured that that purpose is worth it, even if it's discovered by enduring seasons of pain. Higher-level thinkers understand that oftentimes pain is a prerequisite to promotion and that the process is just as important than the end product.

God is always ready to pour out His life-changing revelation upon His people. However, we must ready ourselves to receive what He desires to communicate. Higher-level thinking is not relegated to what is seen. It taps largely into what has not yet come to pass. It takes faith in God to make sure your thoughts are not bound to only what can be seen by the natural eye. There is much about God that supersedes our physical senses of touch, taste, smell, hearing, and sight.

The IM Of Impossible

This new, higher realm of thinking is made possible by the work of Christ on the cross. If you are in Christ you have been made new. The past can no longer hold you at bay. It can only serve as a reference point from which your testimony is built and thanksgiving is offered.

There are two ways you can look at the word impossible. Before I discuss them, allow me to define the term. Impossible denotes that something is not possible, or probable, and can be applied to situations and/or people. It is usually used as an adjective. That means that its primary function is to describe something. Adjectives modify nouns. To modify means to change from its original state, or to change the qualities of something. Satan attempts to use the word impossible to convince you that what God has spoken over your life is incapable of being or becoming true. Since satan is the father of all lies he desires to change the God-ordained state of your life. Operating as a liar means that nothing he says has truth or merit. So, essentially what the enemy does is lie about the truth God tells about you. Satan wants you to consider his version of your story instead of what God has already spoken and will speak.

Satan specializes in over-dramatizing the here and now. He's the master of over exaggeration. Higher-level thinkers don't fall prey to his schemes because they don't worry about the "now." They understand that perseverance, endurance, determination, and faith in God are required to navigate tough circumstances. When satan says, "it can't be done." God usually reminds us of His sovereignty by responding, "Oh, yes it can because I have said it." It is not by our power or might but by His Spirit that we lay hold of every promise. With that in mind, let's take a fresh look at the word impossible.

Look Again

First, I notice that it is really an awesome opportunity for God to show off in your life. Instead of thinking impossible, think, "I'm possible." Take a moment and say it aloud. You fortify your faith by speaking God's blessing upon your life! Always speak where you're going. Don't be ashamed to speak aloud that you are becoming what God has called you to be.

My rationale is this: the only reason God put you here on earth was to be possible for Him. What does that mean? It means that you are released to be all that God has created you to be. Your life is not constrained or limited to what you can't do. It's set free by what you can and will accomplish. You are God's possibility in the most difficult situations. Remember that all things, including you, are possible if you believe.

With higher-level thoughts you can be used by God to be the possibility for someone else's life. You become the answer to someone's prayer because you have the spiritual resources available to truly make a Christ-like difference in their life. Your life shines with the radiance of Christ because you accept what God believes about you. You understand that you aren't defined by your surroundings, but by a loving Heavenly Father who desires that you prosper in all things.

Thinking positive thoughts filled with possibility allows you to experience a greater level of effectiveness and focus. No task is too great. No obstacle is too difficult to overcome. You are an "overcomer" by faith. With total confidence in man comes impossibilities, but with God all things are possible. According to Philippians 4: 13 you can and will do all things through Christ who is your strength [paraphrased].

The second way to consider the term impossible is to extract the prefix "im." Im is a prefix of negative force. It's meaning, derived from Latin, is that of subtraction rather than addition. Im is closely related to the prefixes in and un which also connote lack of ability, influence, or power. Interestingly enough the French form of the prefix in is en which is embedded in the word enemy. Therefore an enemy is a negative force working against the productivity or progress of others.

Another definition of the prefix im equates to "not." For example, if someone called you immature they are in fact suggesting that you are not mature. This is exactly the type of terminology satan thrives on. His desire is to always tell you what you aren't. The devil constantly attempts to badger you with statements like these:

- "You're not good enough."
- "You're not educated enough."
- "You're not thin enough."
- "You're not."
- "You're not."
- "You're not."

On the other hand, God by His Spirit desires to constantly bombard your mind with reminders of who you are in Jesus Christ. Paul's Letter to the Romans, found in the New Testament, is replete with descriptions of who you are in Him. Look at how God describes you.

- You have been justified and redeemed (Romans 3: 24).
- You are set free from the power of sin (Romans 6: 7).
- You are eternally free from condemnation (Romans 8:1).
- You are an heir to God's unlimited riches (Romans 8: 17).
- You are holy because of your connection to Jesus Christ (Romans 11: 16).
- You have been accepted by Jesus Christ (Romans 15: 7).

All of this points right back to Jesus' love for you and His desire to see God's purposes manifested in your life.

In essence, the second way of looking at the word impossible is not a way of looking at it at all. Statements satan makes lead to destruction and death. The statements God makes over our lives are filled with His grace. We qualify to operate abundantly in God's grace because of faith in Jesus Christ. Grace, God's unmerited favor, is necessary so that we can maintain integrity in our thoughts and actions. Higher-level thinking not only propels you into God's favor and abundance, it keeps you there.

chapter eleven
promised place

Ever been excited about going somewhere because you knew that when you arrived it was going to be worth the wait? Whether it's a much-needed vacation or a reunion with a loved one, arriving feels great. Hopes and expectations begin to stir. Emotions manifest in unbridled excitement. The grin is almost unbearable. The closer you get, the more you begin to relish the approaching moment. Similarly, God wants you to be just as excited about the promised place he is drawing you into. He has spent centuries getting where you're headed ready for you. God knows what you've been through to get where you are. He knows better than anyone else what you've sacrificed to even be in a position to advance toward your destiny. God has seen the tears, fear, and uncertainty. Despite your shortcomings, He still desires to bring you into a place of abundance. You are God's child and he takes good pleasure in prospering you spiritually, mentally, physically, and financially.

Your promised place is filled with prosperity, joy, happiness, and peace. Maybe you've been struggling for a while. Those hard times have brought you to your knees. Now you're at the place where you can honestly say you accept God's will, no matter what it entails. Despite what you've been through, be excited because of what God has promised. His promises become increasingly evident as you agree to change, to be different to make a difference. You are God's weapon against satan here on earth. You are God's instrument of peace, love, and joy.

Because we are people of great purpose and promise, God has created us to be a vital part of his arsenal against the enemy. We are change agents. People will be made better because of the life you live and the standards you uphold. In fact, the mind is your greatest weapon. That's why the mind is the most complex part of who we are. Researchers remain baffled at its capability and capacity even after centuries of study and investigation. God made the mind complex for a reason. What results from it-thoughts, ideas, and strategies should change the world. At the genesis of every paradigm-shifting idea is a thought. Those thoughts combine to form ideas. Ideas are transposed into action. Actions get results. That's what you are and will eventually become what you think. Successful people think successful thoughts. Unsuccessful people think unsuccessful thoughts. The mind has the power to shape our lives.

Now that you have allowed the renovation process to shape the way you think, you're ready to help the Kingdom of God advance. God is excited because He now knows that you will serve him and not the lusts of the flesh, which include your own selfish desires.

The Prosperous Place

Prosperity in your promised place means that you possess the authority to improve your spiritual condition. Spiritual growth always leads to financial growth. God desires balance for your life. As you experience financial prosperity God expects to see His desires made evident in the earth. Essentially, you are blessed by God to be a blessing to someone else. The wealth that you accumulate is not only for you, it is for His glory. It's time for Christians to lay claim to all the spiritual and natural resources God desires us to possess. According to His Word Christians can and should be debt-free, own banks, law firms, hotels, television stations, car dealerships, and much more. Understanding God's requirement for blessing frees you from doubting if he will ever give you what you've asked for. If you are connected to God through Jesus Christ, then you are an heir to limitless blessing and favor. The mentality that suggests you will never be successful must die. Thoughts that say you can do and achieve all things through Christ must reside in your thought process.

Destroy "Poor Me"

A renovated mind resists being afflicted by a "poor me" mentality. You have the ability through Jesus Christ to walk into and experience everything God has for you. Don't be scared. Satan strategy is to entrap you in a mindset that snuffs out the possibility of your progress toward prosperity God's way.

Bad Rich

Believe it or not, satan wants you rich too! He desires to use you to build his kingdom of darkness, deceit, and destruction. Satan wants you on his team. However, you should always desire prosperity God's way. God wants you to have an abundance of money and resources. If you came from humble beginnings, thank God that your story didn't end there. Your history is literally His story. Furthermore, God is not finished with you yet. The best is yet to come.

To truly experience your promised place of prosperity you

must change the way you think about money. Money is not evil. The love of money is evil. It's impossible to love God and money at the same time. You must choose one and only one love. God desires a monogamous relationship with you. No cheating allowed. Money will vie for your attention. Money wants your time and all your energy. If money has your undivided attention, God does not. What is greater should always get the best of us.

Greater

By His very nature, God is greater than anything He creates. Money was created by God and therefore doesn't affect him. Money doesn't rule Him. He rules it. Consequently, God never created money to dominate us. We're supposed to exercise dominion over money.

Indeed, God desires for you to have life and to have it more abundantly. A sure way to experience subtraction in your life is to not give God what He is due. Our God is an awesome but jealous God.

Recognize the Source

A renovated mind recognizes that a job is not the source of provision. God is the ultimate source of everything. Your job is really a hobby for which you are compensated. Never depend more on your occupation than God. God is the One who created your job in the first place. God's compensation for your obedience is far more than any job could ever pay. Before you were born you were already hired by God. You are a full-time employee of the Kingdom of God. When the love of Jesus Christ resides in you, the Holy Spirit comes alongside and endorses your efforts. You can get more done in partnership with God's Spirit than without. With the Spirit's guidance and enablement anything can be accomplished for God. When we accomplish great things for God, his way of multiplication invades our lives. The blessings of the Lord make you rich and add no sorrow to your life.

To invite God's supernatural multiplication into your life you must accept His way of doing things. Prosperity is connected to your obedience concerning the finances He has already blessed you with.

Working What You Already Have

Contrary to popular belief, the tithe, which amounts to one-tenth of your gross income, does not invoke a financial blessing from the Lord. The tithe actually protects your finances from satan's diabolical schemes. When you offer your tithes consistently God rebukes satan for your sake. Satan's authority over what God has already provided to you is canceled. The enemy then has no stake or right to liquidate you. Your tithing rebukes the curse of lack and poverty. Tithing takes faith and faith takes you straight into the heart of God.

God expects you to commit your time, talent, and treasures to Him. Giving God ten percent of all our earnings is the least we can do. When we pay the tithe, we support the ministry effort of the local church. Consistent tithing pleases God, prevents the curse of lack, and a major principle of financial prosperity.

Malachi 3:10 teaches that bringing tithes to the church creates substance (resources) to accomplish God's will on earth. In this directive from God are three things every believer should do. First, we are invited to bring our tithes. This implies action on our behalf. This is where many go wrong. The act of bringing implies obedience. When you were a child, and your mother asked you to come to her, either you obeyed her command or resorted to disobedience. Often, bringing your tithe seems difficult because the enemy offers ten-thousand reasons why you shouldn't give God what He deserves. A renovated mind is equipped to ward off satan's mental attacks. It presses forward to do what is right. Satan will never tell you to pay your tithes or give an offering. Instead, he'll cause you to agonize over your financial situation and how the tithe you would give God could be spent in more "productive" ways. Nevertheless, a renovated mind is an obedient mind.

In addition to tithing, we are commanded in Scripture to make offering to the Lord. An offering is any financial gift brought to God over and beyond our tithes. Giving above what is required always pays off. We reap according to what we have sown. Offering your resources to God ensures that whatever you put your hands to will be blessed and prosperous. Psalm 112: 1-3 is an awesome illustration of the result of obedience to God.

> Praise the LORD! Blessed is the man who fears the LORD, Who delights greatly in His commandments. His descendants will be mighty on earth; The generation of the upright will be blessed. Wealth and riches will be in his house, And his righteousness endures forever.

The fear of the Lord is the beginning of all knowledge. God desires that you delight greatly in what He has asked you to do. The resulting fruit of your labor shall be great. That is something to get excited about! There are no limits to what God will do through your renovated mind when it has been obedient by trusting His provision.

A person whose mind is renovated and focused on pleasing God becomes a repository for His wealth and favor. A repository is akin to a storehouse-a treasury or depository. Nothing invites provision more than a depository. Depositories are designed to securely hold vast amounts of fortune. Wouldn't you love for God to trust you to manage millions of dollars for the Kingdom? Your obedience to God paired with a refreshed mindset causes your righteousness (imputed by God) to endure. Righteousness creates a place where God can deposit value assets. Before He places anything of worth in your coffers, God always makes sure it's clean, prepped, and ready for what's coming.

A righteousness life is the setting God seeks before He trusts anyone to govern resources for Him. When family and friends forsake you, your righteousness will endure. When it seems as if the world is caving in, your righteousness shall endure. You are becoming stronger and more equipped mentally and spiritually to complete the assignment God has for your life. The enemy pulled out all the stops in an attempt to cancel God's subscription on your life. Satan's attempts failed. Every time the devil fails, you get stronger and stronger. You derive strength from every victory.

Giving Into Prosperity

The offering you give benefits the Kingdom of God. As you work, the tasks you perform transform lives. Because you are prosperous God's glory can be seen by all. When you are prosperous, God and all who are attached to Him look good! When the work of your hands is prosperous the world has to take note. When you walk in your newness, God is glorified and your fellow brother or sister in Christ is edified.

Spiritual Authority

A renovated mind also allows you to operate in a greater measure of spiritual authority. When you enter places where God is not glorified, you change the atmosphere because of the authority you possess. Have you ever seen someone walk into a room and draw all the attention to themselves? Maybe it was because of what they had on or even their personality. Some people just light up a room and are magnets for attention and adoration. The same can apply in a godly way to believers. We should never enter a situation desiring that people praise us. The authority that God has given is not for our benefit, but so that the causes of Christ are made evident. When we look like vessels of authority demons, devils, and unclean spirits take note. And because God and evil can't co-exist, everything ungodly has to leave. Where there is light darkness cannot hide.

Where light abounds there can be no darkness. Nightfall cannot commence until daytime relinquishes its duty. The great news is that God never goes off duty. He neither slumbers nor sleeps. God will never relinquish His throne!

In Scripture, Jesus at no time is found tolerating the devil. To tolerate something is to permit it to happen. The longer you allow things to happen, the more authority you give away to the opposing person or situation. In Matthew 4 satan attempts to distract and discourage Jesus. The interesting thing is that satan tries to paint Jesus as foolish and naive by using Scripture to justify his requests. Despite having recently finished fasting and praying for forty days and nights, Jesus was still ready for the enemy's attack. If satan quoted Scripture to you, would you be confused? A renovated mind is never fooled by the devil because it knows what God has said in His Word.

A renovated mind is well rehearsed in Scripture, and it knows the difference between the voice of God and the voice of the devil. God always speaks life, while satan speaks death. Actually, satan can't kill you, he can only make you consider killing yourself. The only authority the devil has over your life is what you give him. If you give him an inch he'll take a mile.

A renovated mind enables you to combat the devil with authority given to you by Jesus Christ. Speaking God's Word aloud is a sure way to prevent the devil from executing his plan of destruction for your life. This process is sometimes referred to as making Godly confessions or decrees. Because of what transpired in Eden between God, Adam Eve, and satan we have become prime targets for the Devil. For centuries Christians been targeted by the devil because we are made in the image and the likeness of God. Since before any of us were born, satan has tried to make God look like a fool. However, the wonderful thing is that satan can never win. The flip side is that satan will never quit. He will stop at nothing to make sure that you never experience deliverance from his oppression, discouragement, depression, stress, and distraction. Satan wants you to make the most detrimental decision you could ever make: the choice to be out of intimate relationship with your true source of life and hope, Jesus Christ.

A renovated mind also allows you to live victoriously knowing that no weapon formed against you will prosper. Will adversity come? Yes. Will difficulties arise? Yes. Are you supposed to succumb to the pressures of life? No. Is your purpose defined by current circumstances? No. Is God the beginning and end of all that concerns you? Yes. Take a moment and think back to the worst thing that ever happened to you. Guess what? You survived it! You've been made better and stronger from it and people are blessed because you've made it through difficult times. Your ability to thrive in the midst of adversity is a testament to God's grace and mercy. So let your light shine so that all men can see God's awesome work in your life.

chapter twelve
a greater purpose

God's ultimate goal for renovating your mind is that who He is becomes what you reflect. You were not created devoid of purpose. He knows the beginning from the end. In fact, God is an expert in all things that concern you and your future. He has a greater purpose for your life and mental renovation is a primary means of catapulting you into what he has designed you to do.

His master plan is fool proof. It has no loopholes or escape hatches. God's way is sure and provides security that dispels your deepest and darkest fears. The greater purpose for your life awaits your arrival. The journey may have been long and tedious, but now you stand on the cusp of something fantastic. It is not only your time, but now, it's your turn.

Pieces Of The Whole

Purpose is comprised of three necessary components: determination, confidence, and expectation. All three of these aspects of purpose must operate in great measure so you can truly realize your potential in God. These indispensable traits lead directly into life-changing encounters with God's Spirit, who is eagerly waiting to teach, train, correct, and admonish you.

A Greater Measure Of Determination

Determination arises when the usual just won't do. There arises a sense of urgency that says, "I know things are supposed to be better than this." Determination is fueled by the desire to improve or to progress toward something different. It is birthed from an act of your will. You have to decide to be determined about something. Determination promotes change, often in the way we operate.

The degree to which we are determined is calculated after a situation has been assessed. From that assessment an action plan is developed and implemented. For example, you might assess that you need to shed twenty-five pounds. Once that assessment is processed internally through your thought process, then the external action begins to make that goal a reality.

God is super-determined that you live a life filled with the best he has to offer. God's determination for your life is woven into actions such as: sending his Son Jesus to die for your sins and placing his Spirit within you so that you might live for him.

It should be our consistent goal to be determined about what God deems important. In Psalm 119: 111-112 the Psalmist says,

> Your laws are my treasure; they are my heart's delight. I am determined to keep your decrees to the very end.

Determination must come from the decision to obey God at all costs. Obedience is paramount to God. Disobedience leads into so many adverse situations. Who would want to be disobedient after reading what happened to God's people in biblical times? Someone with a renovated mind is okay with disobeying the predominant sin-filled culture. Our loyalties should rest in God and his principles for abundant living. To disobey satan is to obey God.

Consistent Confidence

As a Child of God you can rest assured that He desires the best for your life. Confidence is birthed from a correct assessment of the past. We often give our past a bad rap because thoughts drudge up memories of people, places, and things that we desire to forget. However, it is rare to forget every detail of the past. I think this is because God desires us to remember the past but not dwell in it. Your past should be a point of reference not a potential stronghold. Why then should we use the past as a reference point? You can't appreciate where you are if you don't know where you've been. Furthermore, you can't perceive a better, more preferred future, if you don't celebrate God for what he has already done for you. Your confidence in God grows as you realize that he has saved and preserved you from dangers seen and unseen. In Psalm 18: 16 -19 David blesses God for delivering him from his enemies.

> He reached down from heaven and rescued me; he drew me out of deep waters. He rescued me from my powerful enemies, from those who hated me and were too strong for me. They attacked me at a moment when I was in distress, but the Lord supported me. He led me to a place of safety; he rescues me because he delights in me.

Who wouldn't feel confident in God after experiencing God like that? But, according to the Scripture God wasn't finished. David goes on to say, "The Lord rewarded me for doing right; he restored me because of my innocence (vs. 20). David was indeed vindicated by the strong hand of God, because he lived upright before him. Keep in mind that David was not a man without fault, however, he was a man submitted to God's will and purposes for his life. As you read through the Bible you'll discover that David made a few more mistakes. Nevertheless, because of the power of repentance and submission to God, David experienced forgiveness and restoration. David is now known for all of eternity as a man after God's own heart (see Acts 13:22).

The combination of God's redeeming love and unparalleled power infuses our lives with the confidence we need to conquer all of life's stressful, mind-polluting situations. It is our job to employ a confident mentality consistently. God takes pleasure in delivering us back into relationship with Himself. When times are hard it's a difficult thing to be confident. When options for a seemingly "easier way" abound, the inclination is to not stick and stay with God, but rather to take the path of least resistance. Operating with a renovated mind causes you to be resolute about believing God no matter how you feel or what you see. The Bible says that everyone doesn't walk by faith, only the just. In fact, the justified can walk in bold faith. You have been justified by Jesus. Take comfort in Jesus' words in Luke 18: 13-14:

> But the tax collector stood at a distance and dared not even lift his eyes to heaven as he prayed. Instead, he beat his chest in sorrow, saying, 'O God, be merciful to me, for I am a sinner.' I tell you, this sinner, not the Pharisee, returned home justified before God. For those who exalt themselves will be humbled, and those who humble themselves will be exalted.

Jesus rebuked those who thought they had it going on. He corrected the big wigs and potentates by decreeing that justification is contingent on our willingness to submit and humble ourselves under God. Our mind, thoughts, and emotions must be satisfied with this newfound confidence in God and not in self. True confidence and boldness comes from remembering your history with God.

Again, David could stand before Goliath boldly because he drew from God's proven track record when he was a shepherd on the backside of the mountain. While no one was watching David dealt with a lion and a bear. Triumph over those circumstances paired faith in God equaled a confidence that defied common understanding and led to overwhelming victory. That same anointing for victory is available for your life through a renovated mind that is confident in God.

Elevated Expectation

We all hold strong beliefs about something. Whether your belief system was developed from an early age or over the last few months, we thrive when we have something or someone to believe in. We typically expect something from what we believe in. As a child, I believed in Santa Claus and expected him to deliver the goods I asked for. The classic Christmas disclaimer said that only good kids would receive gifts from the Big Guy in Red. I, despite my behavioral shortcomings, as a youngster, still expected something great to happen every December 25th.

My expectation didn't end at Santa Claus. I knew that my parents also bought gifts every year for me and my siblings. So, the process of making sure I was on their good side began around October of every year. I had an expectation based on my knowledge of prior Christmases. Every year, without fail, my expectations grew until they became undeniable, or maybe even all-consuming. My parents purchased the toys because they loved me and took pleasure in witnessing me enjoy what they provided.

Likewise, your Heavenly Father takes great joy in providing for you. He said he would supply all your needs according to his vast treasury. That treasury houses much more than money. It's a repository for faith, peace, joy, hope, favor, and love, just to name a few. Our expectations should be based on how good God has been, is being, and shall be to us. His love extends past our present and secures our future. That's why he said in Jeremiah 29:11-14 MSG:

> "I know what I'm doing. I have it all planned out-plans to take care of you, not abandon you, plans to give you the future you hope for. When you call on me, when you come and pray to me, I'll listen. When you come looking for me, you'll find me. Yes, when you get serious about finding me and want it more than anything else, I'll make sure you won't be disappointed..."

Knowing that God passionately loves you and has your every desire in Him at the top of his priority list is exciting. I am ecstatic about what God is doing in your life. Be encouraged and know that you are here for a divinely distinct purpose. Your renovated mind unleashes God's best for your life. When the limits are removed from God because your mind is free to experience Him fully, no one, no thing, no situation, no past event, no future attack can prevent God's glory from being revealed in you.

A New Way To Handle Adversity

God never promised that reaching your purpose would happen without resistance. The purpose of renovating your mind is to eliminate barriers to your success and to retune your perspective. Problems and difficulties wouldn't seem so monumental if we viewed them from God's perspective. That's why it's vitally important to consistently ask God for His revelation so that you can obtain and retain a proper outlook.

Even after you have allowed God to perform His work on your mind, resistance is still sure to present itself. Jesus, the Son of God, realized the resistance that surrounded Him through-out his ministry. However, that resistance wasn't enough to prevent Him from completing the assignment His Father gave him. When Jesus ascended back to heaven He left nothing un-done pertaining to his purpose for coming. It's now our goal to walk in and live out what He left for us. What did Jesus leave? He left us with authority, tenacity, faith, favor, and the list goes on and on. Everything that Jesus left was created to help you reach your highest potential. Bestowal of these things enables you to live victoriously despite external resistance to your pur-pose. The Israelites knew this all too well.

> The enemies of Judah and Benjamin heard that the exiles were rebuilding a Temple to the LORD, the God of Israel. So they approached Zerubbabel and the other leaders and said, "Let us build with you, for we worship your God just as you do. We have sacrificed to him ever since King Es-arhaddon of Assyria brought us here." But Zerubbabel, Je-shua, and the other leaders of Israel replied, "You may have no part in this work, for we have nothing in common. We alone will build the Temple for the LORD, the God of Is-rael, just as King Cyrus of Persia commanded us." Then the local residents tried to discourage and frighten the people of Judah to keep them from their work. They bribed agents to work against them and to frustrate their aims. This went on during the entire reign of King Cyrus of Persia and lasted until King Darius of Persia took the throne (Ezra 4: 1-5).

God's people were in the middle of an expansive construc-tion project when opposing forces decided to apply pressure. The secondary goal of those oppressors was to halt the work of the Lord so that Israel would look weak and feeble. Their pri-mary purpose was to make God look bad. The opposition even made a two-faced offer to assist in the work, even though their true motives were to wreak havoc and dismay.

The story goes that work on the temple came to a halt.

Later, the discovery of a decree to complete the temple from King Cyrus in the archives allowed work to resume under the reign of King Darius. Work was restarted with his orders for all former oppressors to stay away from the process. In fact, King Darius footed the bill from the royal treasury (Ezra 6:4). All things really do work out for those who love the Lord.

All It Takes Is A Word

Everything the Israelites needed to get done had been validated by a decree from the king. Likewise, God wants to decree awesome things over your life. It's His desire that you receive everything He wants you to receive. When God decrees something it is always established. His decrees keep us focused on completing every work He assigns to us. What you must always remember is that God's purpose for your is not just about you. It's about His Kingdom and glory being revealed through us as light in our dark world.

In the quest for greater purpose you must allow yourself to be interrupted by God. Dietrich Bonhoeffer aptly suggests that, "we must not spare our hand where it can perform a service and that we [should] not assume that our schedule is our own to manage, but allow it to be arranged by God." In essence, we're just one part of the masterpiece that the Master is creating to His glory in Jesus' Name. Play your part well and reap the harvest that God has decreed over your life. Greatness of the greatest degree is often manifested during life's most difficult seasons. The mandate from God isn't subject to your surroundings. Examine the life of the Old Testament prophet Elijah. He was called by God to stand and defend even in the midst of major opposition by Ahab and his wife Jezebel. Although, he experienced moments of doubt and fear, God always reassured him that the purpose he was assigned to was fueled by the Power he was connected to. God showed Himself strong at Mount Carmel (see 1 Kings 18) so that all could see and understand that he meant business. With Elijah's mandate from God also came greater responsibility.

Greater purpose means greater responsibility. A renewed mind is prime territory for God to cultivate ideas, strategies, and spiritual warfare that abort all that the devil is engaged in. A renovated mind sees the weakness in satan's plan of attack and exploits that weakness until he is no longer a threat. Your purpose is to dispel the works of darkness. Every attempt of the devil is met with anointed resistance through prayer, scripture study, fasting, and righteousness. You have the authority, because of Christ's victory at Calvary, to reclaim territory for God. You have the right to actively participate in the restoration process of your family and friends. God created you for a specific reason and everything you do for him should be bathed in Scripture-based prayer so that you are mentally available to hear about what's next.

The Next Great Thing

Something wonderful is about to happen. It has been in the works for a while. The process has been well worth the time and effort. The product is worthy of being used to change many. Everything has been set in order and now the time has come. A new way of thinking is now available. It leads to a rewarding life of service to God.

Now, you have the blessed opportunity to impact others for Christ. Your life-change experience will be a process of continuous improvement. Isn't it wonderful that we serve a God who allows us to reap a harvest even while we continue to grow toward Him? With a renovated mind, others can now feast upon God's goodness through you. It was no mistake that He chose you. It was not happenstance that your life has led you this way. Though it has not always been easy, the journey towards mental renewal has been well worth it. God's sacrifice of his son Jesus paired with your desire to move higher undoubtedly leads to a long-lasting, fulfilling life. Go and enjoy the new possibilities a renovated mind affords you.

notes

Chapter Three - Surveying the Strategy

Change Me was an impromptu worship chorus led by guest speaker Bishop Joseph Garlington at the Potter's House in Dallas, Texas in November 2001.

Chapter Four - God Is In Your Mess

What A Friend We Have In Jesus. Lyrics composed in 1855 by Joseph Scriven. Music by Charles Converse to the tune of ERIE. Scriven composed this hymn to comfort his mother who was at great distance from him in Ireland.

Chapter Six - A New Boldness

C.S. Lewis, *See God in the Dock: Essays on Theology and Ethics* (Grand Rapids, MI: Wm. B. Eerdmans, 1970), 101.

Chapter Seven - Dismantling Learned Behavior

This Little Light of Mine. Lyrics by Harry Dixon Loes, musician and teacher. Lyrics were composed in 1920 and are based on Mathew 5: 16.

Chapter Eight - Making Godly Decisions

Dietrich Bonhoeffer, from *Life Together and Prayerbook of the Bible.* (Minneapolis, MN: Fortress Press, 1996). Life Together is a classic in which Bonhoeffer discusses the nature of Christian community.

Jesus Paid It All. Lyrics by Elvina M. Hall. Lyrics were composed in 1865 and are based on 1 Peter 1: 18-19.

Abdullah Birdsong is a devoted servant of God. Chosen by the Lord Jesus Christ to be a trailblazer in His kingdom, Abdullah is a gifted pastor, author, intercessor, entrepreneur, and educator. He holds degrees from Morehouse College and Samford University.

Abdullah's foremost desire is to creatively communicate the Word of God. He is a dynamic change-agent used by God in these last days to prepare, equip, and empower leaders for cutting-edge ministry. Abdullah serves as Lead Pastor of Dunamis Church, a dynamic multi-racial, multi-generational community of believers.

Abdullah is married to Marcia Birdsong and they are the parents of one Samuel Joshua. The Birdsongs reside in Charlotte, North Carolina.

a resource to you

Abdullah is in demand as a leadership consultant, motivational speaker, worship consultant, seminar facilitator, and session musician. Your leaders, youth groups, and students will experience the positive impact of his session long after he is gone. Students have witnessed his high-energy, interactive, and tell-it-like-it-is style at school assemblies, college campuses, youth conferences, and student leadership gatherings.

Churches and ministries throughout the Southeast have also experienced the power of God through Abdullah's ability to present the truths of Scripture in a life-changing and practical way.

To secure Abdullah for your next ministry, leadership, youth, or student event log on to www.abdullahbirdsong.com.

Scan the QR Code below with your smartphone
to access more information*

* To scan the code, download the free reader from www.i-nigma.com